Active Learning across the Content Areas

Authors
Wendy Conklin, M.A.
Andi Stix, Ed.D. and PCC

SHELL EDUCATION

Publishing Credits

Robin Erickson, *Production Director*; Lee Aucoin, *Creative Director*;
Sara Johnson, M.S.Ed., *Editorial Director*; Maribel Rendón, M.A.Ed., *Editor*;
Sara Sciuto, *Assistant Editor*; Grace Alba Le, *Designer*; Corinne Burton, M.A.Ed., *Publisher*

Image Credits

Cover, Getty Images; p.123, Wikimedia Commons; p.148, Wendy Conklin;
all other images Shutterstock

Shell Education

5301 Oceanus Drive
Huntington Beach, CA 92649-1030
http://www.shelleducation.com

ISBN 978-1-4258-1050-4

© 2014 Shell Educational Publishing, Inc.

Active Learning across the Content Areas

Table of Contents

Foreword

I hope you are ready for the refreshing ideas and twists presented by Wendy Conklin and Andi Stix in *Active Learning across the Content Areas*. Not only do they offer teachers an opportunity to target areas that increase discussions, creative thinking, and decision making, but they also provide ways to meet these needs, no matter the content area or grade level. As you begin exploring this book, you will discover that there are great tips on managing an active classroom and group discussions that fill the learning environment as well as explore the benefits to active versus passive learning.

This book could not have come at a better time. As academic rigor increases in states from the demands of standards and assessments, the importance of providing students with opportune times outside of a "sit-and-get" is becoming more important. The brain must be actively involved in the thinking process, not just appear that it is. The ideas that Wendy and Andi share here do just that: they actively engage the brain.

Before truly understanding the brain and how it learns, traditional teaching encompassed mainly the teacher providing verbal and sometimes visual content, with the next action being a worksheet or a page from the textbook. Today, we have had the privilege of learning so much more about active learning and how it improves retention and understanding because of developments in brain research. Engaging students so that they are the creators of meaning is crucial to their long-term success.

In addition, active learning gives teachers an opportunity for ongoing assessments. Imagine this—you conduct one of the activities from this book, perhaps the Mystery Box or Layered Ball Questions, and as you listen in on what students are talking about during the activity, you have a chance to collect information and use what was learned as a formative assessment. Now, take action! Use that information to inform your instruction and scaffold the conversation or questioning to the next level, ever pressing your students forward in their learning.

My hope for you as you read is to experience what I did—the fun of exploring what Wendy and Andi have to offer, trying the ideas with your students, and enjoying seeing their faces light up as they engage in conversation and higher levels of thinking through the implementation of these active learning strategies.

LaVonna Roth, M.S.Ed., M.A.T.
Author of *Brain-Powered Strategies to Engage All Learners*

Chapter

Introducing Active Learning Strategies

"Tell me and I forget. Teach me and I remember. Involve me and I learn."
—Benjamin Franklin

Imagine a classroom where students work intently, some in small groups and some individually. The teacher's expectations are clear, and students have plenty to do. A Magnetic Debate is scheduled for tomorrow, and students are furiously working to gather information to defend their points of view. A few are gathered around primary source documents for close analysis. Others consult computers to verify research information. Some students practice and critique their short speeches. Throughout the week, the teacher is meeting one-on-one with students at their desks to touch base and check for understanding. Later in the week, students will create commercials, write scripts, and practice newscasts that demonstrate what they have learned about the topic. For many teachers, this type of classroom would be intimidating. Will my students stay on task and have anything to show for their group meetings? How would I deal with those who either refuse to work with others or don't contribute positively to the group? Finally, what kinds of grades can I assign to these projects and activities?

As students, many of us might recall writing spelling words five times each along with a sentence. We read the chapter in the textbook, answered the questions at the end of it, took the quiz to see what we could remember, and then forgot the content by the following week. Back then, our well-meaning teachers believed we were learning the material, but we know better today that those teaching strategies decrease student motivation. Although mountains of research tell us that these outdated traditional teaching strategies don't ensure student learning, there are still classrooms that operate in this same fashion.

In any given classroom, a teacher must cover endless amounts of facts, vocabulary, and key concepts that will be tested on end-of-year exams. The stakes are high to pass these tests—not only for students, but for teachers, too. Throughout this process, it is good to be reminded of what is real learning.

The best educators question every tactic they use in their efforts to get students to learn and then seek to design authentic learning experiences for these students. Even so, it is not uncommon to find a teacher who gives students a study guide of genres to take home to study followed by a multiple-choice quiz over the material the following day. If a student aces that quiz, does it mean that he or she learned the material? As educators, we should be asking ourselves if this is the best learning experience we could offer students. Can we do better?

This is also an appropriate time to discuss "performance assessment" and "authentic assessment." We know that formative assessment is when a teacher is helping a student during an activity and that summative assessment is based on grading a student at the end of the unit. Well, authentic assessment is utilized when a teacher-coach assesses how students are working while preparing a task in pairs or in cooperative groups. And performance assessment is how a teacher-coach charts a happening in the classroom while students engage in an active strategy or participate in a simulation, debate, or discussion. How can a teacher chart the experience? We will show you how.

What Is Active Learning, and Why Do We Need It?

Defined, active learning offers an "engagement in learning; the development of conceptual knowledge and higher-order thinking skills; a love of learning; cognitive and linguistic development; and a sense of responsibility or 'empowerment' of students in their own learning" (Lathrop, Vincent, and Zehler 1993, 6). Active learning means that students are engaged in a guided classroom activity instead of sitting quietly and listening to the teacher lecture. A classroom where active learning takes place is one that includes time for collaboration, various forms of communication, and the freedom for movement. This type of classroom demands that students be engaged learners who create knowledge—as opposed to passive ones who only receive information. It also changes the role of the teacher from one who bestows knowledge to a teacher-coach and mentor who acts as a facilitator and provides support and guidance for learning. We are familiar with "hands-on" activities, which much of active learning requires. But active learning also requires "heads-on" activities, meaning the brain is engaged in thinking and creating knowledge through appropriate challenges and peer discussions.

The idea of active learning is nothing new. Even back before many of us were students, Piaget wrote that learners must be active in order to be engaged in real learning (1954, 1974). Piaget was one of several constructivists who believed that students construct their own understanding and knowledge of the world through experiencing things and reflecting on those experiences. For example, when students are presented with new information, they merge it with their previous ideas and experiences. They might change what they think or discard this new information as useless. In effect, they create their knowledge by asking questions, exploring new ideas, and assessing what they know. The emphasis is on the students, not the teacher.

To give a more concrete picture, let's look at a few scenarios in a classroom.

Figure 1.1 Active Learning Scenarios

Active Learning	
Example	**Nonexample**
Students are out of their seats, collaborating with peers on a project.	Students listen to a lecture.
Students use various forms of communication, like podcasting, to share their ideas with others.	Students quietly write responses to questions, using complete sentences.
Students use manipulatives to build models to demonstrate what they learned.	Students work written problems on a worksheet to show what they have learned.
Students create movie trailers to summarize a book they just read.	Students write a one-page book report.
Students participate in small-group discussions in efforts to produce ideas for solving a problem.	Students individually read research material and take notes.
Students use their bodies to act out a scene and demonstrate a newly learned concept.	Students give a two-sentence ticket-out-the-door reflection on what they learned.
Students are presented with higher-order questions that challenge their views and must consult other documents before answering.	Students answer lower-level questions over material they read to ensure basic comprehension.
Students work with primary-source documents to piece together details and clues about an event in history.	Students read a textbook to understand an event in history.
Students design an experiment to test a hypothesis.	Students read a newspaper article about a science breakthrough.

The examples on the left side of the table clearly demonstrate students using heads-on and, in some cases, hands-on activities, while the nonexamples on the right do not demonstrate active learning. At times, teachers need to use the nonexamples like the ones listed in the chart because quick feedback is necessary to know if students are on track in their understandings. The caveat is that these can't be the *only* things students are doing in their day and certainly not the majority of the time. To truly internalize content so students can reference it in the years to come, it is necessary that they experience a wide variety of active strategies.

Active learning, as seen in many of these examples, involves higher-order thinking. If students are to form arguments based on evidence, real thinking is involved. To create something new to show what he or she has learned, higher-order thinking must be used. Students transform from passive thinkers into active ones when they have to defend a viewpoint or look for evidence. When they examine their biases and either change or validate their views with proof, higher-order thinking is taking place. Problem solving while learning to work with others is another example. It is so much easier to be a passive learner. Not much is required, and as a result, not much is produced to ensure long-lasting learning. Active learning, on the other hand, continues to reward students with knowledge and the joy that learning can bring. It grooms them to be lifelong learners.

Being *active* is both mental and physical. To engage students mentally, the tasks must be meaningful, allow for exploration and inquiry, and be student-driven (Mims 2003). The brain needs real contexts to help it organize and connect new information, so it can be recalled later. Some of the best strategies for active learning involve critical thinking, problem solving, and the exchange of ideas. Research shows that these types of tasks motivate students intrinsically and ensure real learning (Mehlinger 1995). The latest brain research explains that the part of the brain—called the cerebellum— that processes movement *also* processes learning. From this, we know that movement and learning constantly interact (Jackson 2009; Willis 2008; Jensen 1998). For example, when we exercise, we build our brain activity. During our workouts, the cerebellum is in high gear. In effect, exercise prepares our brain to respond quickly to challenges. One study showed that students who spent an extra hour each day in gym class outperformed other nonexercising students on exams (Hannaford 1995). Another study showed that aerobic exercise improved short-term memory, a person's reaction time, and creativity (Michaud and Wild 1991). This happens because movement stimulates the brain and makes it active. When a writer feels his brain beginning to stagnate and grow tired, he gets up and moves around to get the blood flowing through his body. This wakes up his mind, and he can generate more writing because of it.

Who Benefits from Active Learning?

It would be difficult to find a population of students for which active learning is not beneficial. What is the reason for this? Everyone can learn by doing. The latest brain research tells us that movement gets the blood flowing to our prefrontal cortex, which helps us think (Hannaford 1995; Jensen 1998). In this state, students are more likely to discover new ideas and make connections. It turns them into active learners who successfully process information instead of passive learners who often miss some important information.

Strategies that involve active learning provide more enjoyable learning experiences for all students. From research, we know that emotions play a large role in learning (McGaugh, Cahill, and Roozendaal 1996). If we can get students to care, then they will be more likely to learn something new and remember it. It provides the motivation for learning while students construct their own knowledge. Through doing this, students discover that learning is hard work, but it is also fun work.

Above all, active learning strategies engage students. Students who are engaged in the content spend more time investigating it (Zmuda 2008). This additional focus and time spent on the curriculum is a bonus for all students, especially those students with special needs. Active learning helps these students stay engaged so that they will learn more and at a quicker pace.

No matter what the academic ability, all students benefit from active learning strategies. The majority of active learning situations are open-ended, which appropriately provides the challenge that above-grade-level students need. Struggling learners are provided hands-on opportunities that make the content accessible to them. Content becomes more interesting, and there is an intrinsic motivation to understand it. Active learning provides English language learners opportunities for language use and vocabulary development since so many of these strategies involve communication and group work. The content becomes more meaningful to these students because they become active participants. The potential for each learner is endless and is only restricted to what each individual student can do, making it a perfect way to scaffold instruction in the classroom.

Active Learning = Multimodal, Multiple Intelligences, and Differentiation

Active learning connects the visual, spoken, auditory, literary, and linguistic modes of instruction. Students come to our classes with varying strengths and weaknesses. Because there are many ways to handle the information in an active learning environment, it taps into students' strengths while also helping them overcome their weaknesses. For example, during any given class, students write and deliver speeches, examine documents, paint images, or act out scenes. They speak, listen, and collaborate with one another and learn how to work with their peers in the process. As a result, this multimodal approach helps more students develop a better understanding of the content (Baker 1989; Willingham 2009).

Multiple intelligences often come to mind when speaking of multimodal activities. This theory of learning is based on the work of Howard Gardner (1993). He has identified eight intelligences, which include verbal/linguistic, logical/mathematical, bodily/kinesthetic, intrapersonal, interpersonal, musical/rhythmic, visual/spatial, and naturalist. He says that everyone possesses each of these intelligences, but some intelligences are more developed in each of us than are others. Teacher-coaches can plan classroom activities to support these intelligences and thus make the content more engaging and attractive to the various learners in a classroom. For example, by introducing content visually, spatially, and kinesthetically, more students will fully grasp that content because it aligns with how they learn best. Another example would be giving students the choice to produce a song (musical), a diary (linguistic and intrapersonal), or a map (visual/spatial) to show what they have learned. Teacher-coaches are more likely to receive better quality and clarity of work because learning styles are taken into account.

Differentiation is a key component of active learning strategies. Because many of the activities are open-ended, active learning strategies differentiate for all learners. For example, most questions used in these activities are open-ended, meaning that there is not just one correct answer. With these types of questions, even the brightest students can be challenged to think to their potential. Having group support during many of the activities helps scaffold the content for struggling learners. Knowing that they can collaborate with their peers in small groups helps build their confidence before presenting to an entire class. For other students, having to work in small groups may challenge their social skills, and they must learn techniques for compromising and getting along with others—both valuable skills for the workplace. In this sense, the teacher-coach instructs students on how to productively work together by using coaching techniques.

Many of the products students produce support various learning styles and thus are differentiated. The teacher-coach can easily apply different levels of support to these activities, too. For example, during an Identity Crisis activity, some students can use a modified help sheet to give them support to form good questions while trying to guess their identity. To give the right amount of challenge, the teacher-coach can change directions for various students as to what can and cannot be placed on their Mystery Boxes. The general idea is to provide the right amount of challenge for students with varying abilities.

Making These Strategies Work for You

When some teachers hear the words *active learning strategies*, they worry that they will have to set aside several days to a week for these strategies. While a few active learning strategies will take several days from beginning to completion (such as the Lobbyist Hearing), there are plenty of these strategies that can be done within a normal day of instruction (like the Layered Ball activity). If these strategies help students to internalize and remember content, then they are worth doing on a daily basis when possible.

Remember, no active learning strategy has to be done exactly as explained in this book. Teacher-coaches should modify components of these activities to fit their classroom needs. For example, Mystery Boxes can be assigned as homework. Some strategies, like the Identity Crisis, serve as great assessment pieces, both formative and summative. There is no reason why these activities can't be a refreshing change from the traditional pencil-and-paper test if they concretely show what students do and do not know about a topic. Do what works best for your students and your class will become student-centered as the strategies will reflect an environment authentic to their needs.

Making Space for Active Learning

Some teacher-coaches feel they don't have enough space to conduct active learning. But not all active learning strategies require a lot of space for movement. For example, many require small-group discussions in which students might need to change seats with others in the class. Students move around to participate during Layered Ball Discussions. The strategies that do require more space are kinesthetic in nature; students use their bodies to demonstrate what they have learned.

Many classrooms are cramped with bodies or are just small in size and don't allow for much movement. Sometimes, teacher-coaches will need to make small adjustments like scooting furniture to the side of the room for a class period. Strategies such as Carousel Brainstorming can be done by moving students to the hallways if enough space isn't available in the classroom. Other activities can be accommodated by using outdoor spaces or, if possible, switching classrooms for a day with a teacher who has a larger one. Some principals allow teachers to use an auditorium or a cafeteria. The key is to think flexibly for ways to incorporate these strategies with your particular classroom design.

Confidence in Managing Active Classrooms

With such an active classroom, how does a teacher-coach make sure that everyone participates and that certain students don't distract from class discussions or work? One key element to think about is seating arrangements. We should use what we know about our students to design the best seating arrangements because their location in the classroom has everything to do with how students participate.

The teacher-coach first needs to get to know the students by observing how they act during classroom activities. For example, auditory learners need to be near you, visual students need to be closer to the board or wherever the "action" takes place, and quiet students need to be in a place where they can have your ear to quietly voice their ideas. Students who are likely to distract others should have a good view of your instruction but be out of the view of other students. Language learners need to sit near students who are helpful, patient, and willing to offer language support when needed. Lastly, students who contribute positively to discussions should be in locations where they can influence others.

It will take many efforts of adjusting and rearranging until you find what works in your classroom. Even then, dynamics will change depending on the activity. The key is to pay acute attention to where students perform best. How to manage groups within the classroom will be explained in the following chapter. Strategies will change depending on the needs of the class.

Active Learning Is in Style

The key to getting our students to learn is to provide experiences where they can make meaning for themselves. Remember what we learned long ago about students constructing their own knowledge? In education, philosophies of teaching come and go. Depending on the needs at the time, the focus changes. When something does come back into focus, new knowledge is gained on how to do it better. We see how it ties to the other things we've been focusing upon. Strategies that support active learning are nothing new. But luckily, we are being reminded that students need these strategies to help them learn. Since the latest brain research coupled with our own observations give us clues into how our students' minds learn information, we can now begin designing authentic learning experiences for our students.

The Role of the Teacher-Coach in Active Learning

In the past, teachers have been defined as facilitators. But today, the new defined role of a teacher is one of a coach who offers inspiration, guidance, and training and one who enhances students' abilities through motivation and support (Stix and Hrbek 2006).

The goal of a teacher-coach is to increase student success by helping students:

- find their inner strengths and passions in order to nurture self-worth and identity;
- have a voice in their own learning and negotiate collectively with the instructor to create the goals and objectives;

- passionately engage in discussion about content to increase memory retention and fuel motivation to learn; and

- use their inner talents to bring their work to the highest level of scholarship attainable.

The coaching strategies, which have been used successfully in some of the most diverse classrooms in the United States, can help to:

- empower individuals by allowing them ownership of their work;

- improve organizational and note-taking skills;

- overcome emotional and environmental challenges;

- resolve conflicts; and

- ensure harmonious group or team work.

The teacher as coach has the determined objective of having students find their own way within a given structure. The teacher-coach encourages students to attain the learning skills needed to move on to a higher level of achievement while realizing their academic potential (Kise 2006). It allows students to work freely within a given structure so that they become more independent and authentically produce work as it relates to the content studied (Crane 2002). This philosophy parallels Charlotte Danielson's Framework, which many states are using as a basis for teacher evaluation (Danielson 2011).

So let's take a look at some of these strategies that make the teacher as coach such a powerful approach that increases motivation and self-esteem in our students. We will examine:

- Negotiable Contracting of Assessment

- The GOPER Model

- The 3Ps & C Model

- The 3-Step Reflective Process

Negotiable Contracting of Criteria for Assessment

Assessment is a key part of instruction in any of today's classrooms. The results of assessments should be used to inform instruction and support students' future learning. It is important for students to understand how they will be assessed in order to truly allow them ownership over their learning. Negotiable contracting is a terrific way to get students involved in setting the criteria on which their grades will be determined. It is a technique that asks students to help the teacher establish the criteria that will be used to assess an assignment. Adaptable to all content areas and flexible enough to accommodate most types of learning, negotiable contracting is currently being implemented in many classrooms.

Teacher-coaches may at first be wary of asking students for input for their assessment, fearing that they may take advantage and set very low standards. This seldom occurs; rather, when asked to suggest assessment criteria, students are surprisingly responsible and thoughtful (Stix 2002). Students who are appropriately coached can often pinpoint just what they think is important to learn in a given unit.

Allowing students to help set assessment criteria makes them more willing to accept responsibility for the grades they receive, and it motivates them to do the best they can to meet their own goals. They do not view grades as arbitrarily bestowed gifts or punishments. If a student gets a grade of 86 out of 100 on a project, he or she can refer to the list of criteria and their respective values to see exactly why 14 points were deducted. With this understanding, students are better able to critique both themselves and one another.

Determining Assessment Criteria During Negotiable Contracting

Once the teacher coach has described in detail the strategy to be used, follow these steps to support the implementation of negotiable contracting:

1. Ask students to imagine that they are the teacher and that they will be creating a list of criteria that should be used for assessing one another's scholarly work and ability to speak and behave properly during the simulation.

2. Have students work individually to create their own lists.

3. Divide students into cooperative groups and allow them to share their ideas and consolidate their lists to five criteria.

4. Have group members arrange the five chosen criteria in order of importance hoping that they will be the first to share an essential idea.

5. Call on a spokesperson from a group to submit one idea and record that idea on a sheet of chart paper.

6. Repeat this process, rotating from group to group. Once an idea is listed, another group may not restate it. Allow students to use a check mark on their lists for ideas shared by other groups. This skill is called *active listening*.

7. If the students have not thought of a certain criterion that you think is important and meaningful, add the item to the list and explain your reasoning to the class.

8. List the results on a large sheet of chart paper as a reference guide, and post the chart in a visible area of the classroom.

9. Discuss and negotiate with students which of the criteria are most salient, and agree on four or five of the criteria to use for assessment.

Sample suggestions for a class debate or discussion may be:

- Actively speaks and participates in discussion that demonstrates the understanding of the case
- Responds to another speaker who demonstrates comprehension of subject matter
- Asks quality questions that demonstrate logical thought
- Refers to his or her notes or any text with pertinent information
- Discusses the topic critically and tries to evaluate the topic from the particular time period

10. The final list is organized in order of importance. Discuss how much each criterion is worth. For example, you may decide that proper research should be weighted more heavily than eye contact during a presentation.

11. For long-term tasks, work with students to draft rubrics.

Once the negotiation is completed, the work can begin. Of course, some lessons may not lend themselves as readily to negotiated assessment because they may be short "Do Now" lessons or reflection strategies, so there are times when digging this deep isn't required.

The GOPER Model

A favorite coaching model used in the classroom is the GOPER Model of problem solving (pronounced GO-pher). This model can be used with many active learning activities. Not only is this a great model for the teacher-coach to use with students, but cooperative groups can also use it amongst themselves. On a large scale, for example, the class can brainstorm putting together a museum of butterflies. They can use the model to determine the overall goal for what the exhibit will look like as people enter the space. The GOPER Model can also be used to help students write their research papers for a chosen topic and determine what artifact they want to design for the display. Many teachers create a class poster of the model for referencing.

The coaching process can be broken down into five stages for class, group, or individual work. Teacher-coaches should help students to:

G = Focus on the *goal*

O = Understand their *options*

P = Create and implement a *plan*

E = *Eliminate* roadblocks

R = *Reflect* on what they accomplish.

GOPER Stage 1: Focusing on the Goal

The art of the teacher-coach lies in bringing awareness to students and focusing their attention. By using the questions and comments below, teachers can help their students figure out what they want to accomplish rather than simply telling them what to do.

When students figure out their goals for themselves, they feel a sense of ownership.

- Describe your goal in detail.

- What specifically are you planning to accomplish?

- Now that you know the situation, explain in detail what you will do to change it.

- Which problem, that affects you the most, do you want to focus on solving?

- What do you most urgently want to change?

We recommend that the teachers start by asking general questions and then hone in on more specific ones. The more information students uncover by themselves, the more attention they will pay to the task. Let's examine how Ms. Rutchik follows the five steps of the GOPER Model in assisting her student groups from the previous scenarios.

Ms. Rutchik: Tell us a bit more about why you would like to do a Quaker settlement [*focusing on the goal*]. What is special about the Quakers that make them different from other colonial groups?

Vikas: They helped runaway slaves.

Olivia: We all read about Harriet Tubman and the Underground Railroad last year. The Amish left their country, just as my family left China.

Ms. Rutchik: Describe in detail what sets them apart from other colonists and communities in America.

Vikas: Quakers are like the Amish that live in the Pennsylvania Dutch country.

Ryan: They're cool. They don't fight, and they don't make war. They're against killing.

Pedro: Since my family came from Colombia, I guess it would be interesting to learn about others who came to the United States. People from our church really helped us.

Ms. Rutchik: This is not an easy task, but I like how you are discussing it together. I like to see you all cooperating and contributing. What will you need to do?

Olivia: We'll have to read about the Quakers. We can use some of the books at the workstation.

Ms. Rutchik: Your written reports together with the site plan will really result in an excellent project. What would you like to focus on that you think is very important for making your site plan [*focusing on the goal*]?

Ryan: We know the Quakers were a religious group.

Pedro: They probably got chased out of where they lived because of their religion.

GOPER Stage 2: Understanding the Options

Teacher-coaches need to let groups determine their options for themselves rather than impose a course of action on them. Ownership is paramount here. When a group falters, the coach should guide students to a better understanding of available options rather than simply taking over. Once students have exhausted their own list of options, the teacher can ask them if he or she may offer some additional help. Teacher-coaches can use the following statements and questions to guide students while also ensuring that they retain a sense of ownership:

- That's one option—what's another?

- Generate a list of the resources you will need to make your position believable.

- Of the resources that you described, which would be the most effective? You can't choose all of them, so which are your top choices?

- In what ways will others respond to each of your choices during the discussion?

The following vignette shows how Ms. Rutchik helped her students to understand their options.

Ms. Rutchik: Describe how the materials at the workstation helped you with your site plans.

Olivia: Some are good, but other books at the workstation are difficult to read.

Ms. Rutchik: Okay, then we'll work on finding books that are more suitable. I'm still glad that you are making the effort. I'm pleased that everyone is trying to get good information for your project [*understanding the options*]. Where could you get other books that might be easier to handle?

Ryan: I'll check my neighborhood library, but those books are sometimes just as hard.

Olivia: A lot of the books at the library aren't specifically about Quakers, and it isn't easy getting the information that we'll need.

Ms. Rutchik: What can you do to make your work and your reading less difficult [*understanding the options*]?

Vikas: Ryan can bring in the books from the library, and I'll check out the Internet. We can bring in all the books and stuff that we can find and look through them together.

Olivia: If they have lots of pictures, that would help and make things easier.

Ms. Rutchik: You're all doing a terrific job in getting information, and your colonial site plan will reflect all of the work you're doing. When you check out the internet, Vikas, be sure to check your sources. Many of the libraries that specialize in historical archives may be of use to you.

GOPER Stage 3: Creating and Implementing a Plan

When students list their tasks in order of importance, they can visualize a reasonable plan. Having a plan helps decrease students' anxiety levels because it allows them to work within a logical framework. To coach students through the prioritizing stage, teachers might ask the following:

- Create a plan of action that will help you achieve your goals. First, write down all the things that you need to do. Once you have your list, place the items in a logical order for completion. Now that you have a plan, each one of you will have to take on responsibility in an equitable manner.

- What is your timeline? What comes next? How can you work out a plan?

- What roles will you assign to each person so that the task will be completed?

- What materials do you need or have? Describe the materials at the workstation that are suitable.

It is important to understand that the teacher-coach's responsibility is not to resolve the problems that students encounter but rather to guide students through their questions in a way that encourages them to solve the problems on their own.

Returning to Ms. Rutchik's class, let's see how she helps her students to create and implement a plan of action.

Ms. Rutchik stayed close to the groups and monitored their activities over the next few days. She was especially interested in how Vikas, Olivia, Ryan, and Pedro were pursuing their research.

Ms. Rutchik: I see you've brought in some new books and that you found the materials that were added to the workstation. I'm glad to see that you all have your heads together and that you're carefully discussing all your information.

Ryan: We have lots of information, but we don't know how we want to use it.

Vikas: We found some pictures that showed early Quaker settlements. That helped us at times more than any of the reading.

Ms. Rutchik: You made a good start gathering information. So what comes next [*creating and implementing a plan*]?

Pedro: Everyone wants to write a report on farming because that's what most of the information we found was about.

Ryan: There was other stuff, mostly about religion.

Pedro: But none of us found it interesting.

Olivia: That's not true. I think the Quakers' religion was cool. They didn't have priests. There were no rituals and ceremonies. If anyone did something wrong, they stood up at the meeting house and said so to the whole community.

Ms. Rutchik: How can you work out a plan that lets you know who will be writing the research sections?

Vikas: Well, Olivia likes the religion, so if she wants to write a report on that, I have no problem.

The next time Ms. Rutchik checked on the group, Vikas, Olivia, Ryan, and Pedro had listed everything that had to be done.

GOPER Stage 4: Eliminating the Roadblocks

Teacher-coaches should first help students probe for obstacles that may not be obvious to them. Then, they should ask the students for permission to share certain views with them. At this point, teachers can point to certain obstacles and ask the students to think about ways to prepare for them, using statements and questions such as the following:

- Explain in detail what you will need to do to avoid this roadblock.

- Place yourself in someone else's shoes, and try to solve the challenge from his or her perspective.

- Who could help you avoid this roadblock?

- Describe specifically what action you took and what the effect was. Were any of your actions met with a negative response? If so, which ones, and how did you overcome the negative response?

The teacher-coach needs to be objective and make certain that prejudicial attitudes or judgmental opinions never come into play during the give-and-take with students. Phrasing such as, *Why on Earth did you do that?* is both provocative and harsh and can make students embarrassed and defensive. Instead, teacher-coaches should use phrasing such as, *I'm curious, what led you to make that decision?* or *What can we learn from this?* It is a rule of thumb that the teacher-coach should use as little evaluative language as possible.

The following vignette from Ms. Rutchik's class shows her helping Vikas's group to eliminate roadblocks.

Ms. Rutchik noticed that Ryan was not pleased; his chair was turned away, and he was slouching and hanging his head. Ms. Rutchik observed that Ryan's peers were ignoring him.

Ms. Rutchik: Can I join in for a little while, and see what the group is working on? I'm sensing a disconnect here. What is keeping Ryan from wanting to be involved right now?

Vikas: We're trying to find a location for the Quaker meeting house.

Ms. Rutchik: What challenges are you experiencing?

Olivia: Ryan keeps insisting it should be a building with a steeple.

Pedro: He wants to put a big church smack in the middle of the settlement.

Ryan: Well, the Quakers were an important religious group, weren't they?

Pedro: We're trying to tell him that Quakers didn't have a church.

Vikas: Right. They had a meeting house, which is a different kind of building.

Ryan: But why can't it have a steeple, like any church? I thought they were Christians.

Ms. Rutchik: Who can help Ryan understand why his idea for a Quaker meeting house with a steeple might be inappropriate for your settlement [*eliminating the roadblocks*]?

Olivia: The Quakers were different from Catholics and other Christian groups.

Ms. Rutchik: Tell us more, Olivia.

Olivia: Steeples were used to echo the grand churches in Europe. The Quakers were against all the glitz. They wanted things simple without all the rituals, without the grandeur.

Ryan: Oh, I didn't know that.

GOPER Stage 5: Reflecting

In the last GOPER stage, students think about and reflect on what they've accomplished, so they can move forward or even repeat the process again. The teacher-coach poses open-ended questions that urge students to reply with detailed descriptions. The goal of this stage is to encourage students to become more self-aware by comparing their levels of development before and after the activity. Coaches can use questions and statements such as the following:

- How well do you think you accomplished what you set out to do?

- Describe in detail what you learned.

- In reflection, what do you need to add to your plan that you didn't originally consider? A plan that is worked from beginning to end without modification is too rigid. In what ways do you want to change your plan to meet your expectations more effectively?

Let's return to Ms. Rutchik's class and see how she coaches the students to reflect on their accomplishments.

The next day, when everyone had finished their work, Ms. Rutchik approached Vikas's group.

Ms. Rutchik: I liked the way you pulled together when the need arose. I also like how you overcame your difficulties. How well do you think you accomplished what you set out to do [*reflecting*]?

Vikas: I thought we had a good plan to follow.

Ryan: We picked the topic of the Quakers that we were all interested in doing.

Olivia: The hardest part was deciding on the cutouts and where to put everything on our site plan.

Vikas: Yeah, but we cooperated and agreed. We only argued a bit.

Ryan: It was good that we all shared the jobs and the work. It made it a lot easier.

Pedro: I found the coloring boring.

Ryan: Yeah. Too much time coloring every part of the contour map.

Vikas: But look how nice it looks. It makes the Quaker settlement look real with all the beautiful colors.

Ms. Rutchik: So you felt that you worked well together, and you like the end result, but coloring the site plan was a bit too much. At what point did you feel that you needed more support [*reflecting*]?

Vikas: I found that some of the books were difficult.

Pedro: But the books you brought after we talked were very helpful.

At the end of the activity, each group gave an oral presentation explaining how it created its settlement and upon what information it based its construction. Each group spoke for a few minutes, explaining what made its colonial settlement different from the others in North America. After each presentation, the group answered questions from the class.

For Ms. Rutchik and her entire class, the site-planning lesson was a challenging and enjoyable learning experience. All of the groups encountered more or less the same problems as Vikas, Olivia, Ryan, and Pedro—minor pitfalls that they always confronted and gradually surmounted and that sometimes even propelled them forward. By having the groups create nine separate settlement plans with an oral presentation and question and answer session for each, Ms. Rutchik enabled her students to gain a truly comprehensive overview of "the Peopling of America."

GOPER Assessment Form

Teacher-coaches can use the form in Figure 1.2 to assess group progress at each GOPER stage. The form also serves as a reminder for teachers to revisit specific groups and follow up on issues of concern. Teachers can modify the form for use with different types of assignments. A full-size version of the form can be found in the appendix.

Figure 1.2 **The GOPER Assessment Form**

The GOPER Assessment Form

Names of Students, Team Name, or Table Number:

Topic:

G: Has the group established their goal(s)? What is their goal or are they still brainstorming?
Date:

Date:

O: In what ways do they have a good comprehension of their options?
Date:

Date:

P: Describe in detail their plan of action:
Date:

Date:

E: Do they have any roadblocks, and if so, describe specifically how they are handling them:
Date:

Date:

R: Explain whether or not the group examines and reflects upon their actions as they move along. In what ways did they learn from working with one another or from accomplishing this project or task?
Date:

Date:

	Goal	Options	Plan of Action	Eliminate the Roadblocks	Reflection
Dates Completed					

Comments and Reminders:
Date:

Date:

The 3Ps & C Model

This specific model in coaching is not just designed to give students assistance but to respect their autonomy. When students feel that they own their own work, their motivation increases. This method allows the teacher-coach to approach a cooperative group or a specific student in a way that honors their right to make their own decisions.

Permission

Purpose

Positive Suggestion or Support

Compliment

The following scenario shows the 3Ps & C Model as it is used in Ms. Rutchik's class.

Ms. Rutchik: May I join you for a few minutes [*permission*]? I would like to hear about your site-plan project [*purpose*]. I know you all have the necessary abilities and that you can be creative. I'm sure that you can make your colonial site a success, as you've done on previous projects [*positive suggestion/support*].

Vikas: I think we'll do okay. So far, we work well together.

Ms. Rutchik: What is the most important thing you have to determine before starting this project [*purpose*]?

Ryan: We have to decide what group we want to be. We also have to decide where to build our colonial site.

Pedro: We all have some ideas; but at this point, we can't agree.

Ms. Rutchik: What might be behind the lack of agreement?

Olivia: We don't have much specific information, but we've done the assigned readings. I guess we haven't shared enough with one other.

Ms. Rutchik: I saw all the preparatory work that you've done, and I was pleased to see everyone working together. I also liked that everyone took notes as they did their readings from the workstation. You're making headway and moving in the right direction [*compliment*]. What choices are you considering?

Pedro: Puritan, Quaker, and Huguenot.

Ms. Rutchik: Now that we have them listed, what specific qualities make each of them unique? Once you've discussed how they differ, then you might be able to come to a decision.

As described above, the teacher-coach was invited into the group in a non-forceful manner. It set the tone for a coaching environment and helped to facilitate the group's discussion so that they could eventually make a choice for their project.

The 3-Step Reflective Process

There are always moments when students hit a wall and are suddenly confronted by a problem that seems impossible to solve. In such situations, teacher-coaches can come to the rescue with the 3-Step Reflective Process. During this process, the teacher-coach works with the student to reflect upon similar instances in the past; determine what course of action was successful then, and why; and consider how to apply a similar solution to the current problem.

Teacher-coaches can use the following questions and statements to guide students through the three steps:

Step 1: Reflect on Similar Instances in the Past

- Might there be something in the past that was similar to what you are currently dealing with?

- Please share how you were able to solve the problem at that time.

Step 2: What Elements Were Successful?

- For what reasons did the solution previously work well?

- Describe specifically some elements that worked.

Step 3: Application to Current Situation

- Explain specifically how you think you can apply your prior knowledge to your current situation.

- Describe in detail any powerful information from your previous experience that can now be applied.

- What are some resources that will help you achieve your current goal?

To see how the 3-Step Reflective Process works, let's travel to Mrs. Gurny's science classroom.

Mrs. Gurny has noticed that Isabella, usually an actively involved student, is focusing her attention beyond the classroom window. Though she occasionally brings her attention back to the class, overall she appears unfocused and uninterested.

Mrs. Gurny: Isabella, you were assigned to read the section on how hydroelectric power is generated, but it appears that you are focused elsewhere.

Isabella: I didn't understand the textbook. I get frustrated when there aren't any pictures or diagrams.

Mrs. Gurny: Could it be because you're a visual learner?

Isabella: Well, I don't know about that, but art is my favorite subject.

Mrs. Gurny: Fine, Isabella. In your other classes, when you don't understand the text, what do you do to help yourself? *[Step 1]*

Isabella: Well, in math class, I like to use those fun materials—the canisters—for algebra.

Mrs. Gurny: Please explain. Tell me why that helps you.

Isabella: I pretend that the x is hidden inside the canister. I can see what the algebraic expression means.

Mrs. Gurny: Once you no longer have the need to use the cans, how do you finish your class work and complete your homework assignments? *[Step 2]*

Isabella: I draw them in my notebook. After a while, I don't need the drawings, but they help me out in the beginning to understand what I'm doing.

Mrs. Gurny: How could you apply your special artistic talent here, in science class? *[Step 3]*

Isabella: I haven't given it much thought, but I could try to draw a picture as I read each section in the text.

Mrs. Gurny: That's a great idea, and I think it will work.

Isabella: But what do I do if I get confused and stuck?

Mrs. Gurny: Don't worry, Isabella. I'll keep an eye on you as I oversee the class. If I see that you're having difficulties, I'll come over and help. If you're pleased with your drawings when you're finished, do you think we could use them as a model for the class to help the others understand hydroelectric power?

Isabella: Sure!

Let's Think and Discuss

1. Describe in detail some active learning strategies that you already use in your classroom.

2. In what ways could you use some help with regards to active learning?

3. What might be the biggest obstacle to incorporating more active learning in your classroom?

Chapter

Active Learning for All Students

While we can confidently paint a broad brushstroke and say that active learning is for everyone, there are specific benefits for certain populations of students. The active learning strategies presented in this book support various learning styles. These strategies also open the doors to thinking deeply and using higher-order thinking skills as the Common Core State Standards mandates (CCSS 2010). But to be successful with all students, differentiation often becomes necessary. With just a little bit of know-how and a few adjustments, active learning strategies can easily be differentiated so that all students will be challenged appropriately. English language learners also benefit from active learning because the discussions and questioning techniques give them a place to develop their language more fully.

Learning Styles

Active learning strategies tailor activities according to the diverse learning styles of students. Using different strategies presented in this book on a regular basis offers a wide range of opportunities for all learners. Students will feel confident doing things they are good at while also taking on the challenge of doing things that are not second nature.

The multiple intelligences model is based on the work of Howard Gardner (1983). Many educators have come to think of multiple intelligences as a philosophy of how children learn. It provides avenues by which all students can achieve success. Sue Teele (1994) from the University of California, Riverside, sums up Gardner's goal of the multiple intelligences model by saying that "multiple intelligences provide for different windows into the same room. We need to unleash the creative potential in all our schools in order to open as many windows as possible for every student in every classroom to succeed" (152). She concludes by emphasizing that "the future mandates that we all move forward together in a way that builds on both our mutual strengths and respects our unique differences" (142).

The active learning strategies presented in this book support students' multiple intelligences. Kinesthetic learners need opportunities for movement within the learning environment. They thrive and make better connections to the content when movement is involved. Many active learning strategies also meet the needs of visual-spatial learners by giving them the visual stimulation that allows these students to learn at their maximum level. Musical rhythmic learners thrive with strategies that help them make sense of the content through music. Verbal linguistic learners have the opportunities for writing and delivering speeches and defending their points of view through prepared discussions. Students with strong interpersonal learning styles interact with others for discussions, debates, production of art, plays, and projects. On the other hand, students have plenty of opportunities for reflection and individual work that those who thrive on an intrapersonal learning style need. Logical mathematical learners benefit from putting together arguments that can prove a point or a side to the story. Analyzing materials also strengthens students' logical-thinking skills.

To find out your students' multiple intelligence strengths and select active learning strategies that will work best for your students, you can have students fill out an inventory like the Multiple Intelligences Inventory seen below (Conklin 2004). Each section represents a different multiple intelligence. Scoring high in a section indicates a student's preference or strength.

Section 1—Verbal/Linguistic Intelligence

Section 2—Logical/Mathematical Intelligence

Section 3—Rhythmic/Musical Intelligence

Section 4—Visual/Spatial Intelligence

Section 5—Bodily/Kinesthetic Intelligence

Section 6—Interpersonal Intelligence

Section 7—Intrapersonal Intelligence

Section 1—Verbal/Linguistic

Do you like to write poetry or stories? _____

Do you have a journal or a diary that you write in? _____

Do you like solving crossword puzzles or creating tongue twisters? _____

Do you enjoy debating? _____

Would you like to write a script for a TV show? _____

Would you enjoy telling stories to a younger class? _____

Section 2—Logical/Mathematical

Do you enjoy solving math problems and/or analogies? _____

Do you like to play counting games? _____

Do you enjoy writing math story problems? _____

Do you like to play checkers or chess? _____

Do you like finding measurements for things? _____

Do you enjoy making graphs to show information? _____

Section 3—Rhythmic/Musical

Would you enjoy writing an advertising jingle for a product? _____

Do you play an instrument? _____

Is it easy for you to think of sound effects to make a story more interesting? _____

Do you pick up tunes and rhythms easily? _____

Would you ever like to write your own song? _____

Do you enjoy going to concerts? _____

Section 4—Visual/Spatial

Do you like putting together puzzles? _____

Do you enjoy drawing or painting? _____

Would you like creating or reading a map of your neighborhood? _____

Do you like playing board games? _____

Would you like to create a video of an important event? _____

Would you ever want to design a sculpture? _____

Section 5—Bodily/Kinesthetic

Do you enjoy playing sports? _____

Would you ever want to learn sign language? _____

Do you like exercising or hiking? _____

Do you enjoy acting out plays? _____

Do you feel like you need to move your body all the time? _____

Do you enjoy dancing? _____

Do you like to create signals with your body to remember things? _____

Section 6—Interpersonal

Do you like playing games with friends? _____

Do you enjoy doing class work with a group of people? _____

Would you want to interview someone important? _____

Do you like conducting surveys? _____

Are you good at solving problems between people? _____

Do you like being around lots of people? _____

Section 7—Intrapersonal

Do you keep a diary or a journal? _____

Do you like setting goals for yourself? _____

Do you spend time thinking about your work? _____

Would you ever like to write an autobiography? _____

Do you spend lots of time thinking quietly? _____

Do you need to spend time alone every day? _____

(Adapted from Conklin 2004)

times, some students need support or differentiation, so they can
...ipate fully in an activity. Differentiating the process by which students
...ipate becomes necessary, so all students can benefit from active learning.
...examine the Negotiations and Settlements strategy. In this forum,
...nts work in cooperative groups. Two students representing one point
...ew try to negotiate a settlement with two other students representing a
...rent point of view. This can be done in science, for example, where pairs
...discuss the use of genetic testing to diagnose cancer. While reading a
...in language arts, pairs can represent characters with differing opinions
...are asked to come to terms with their differences.

...o begin this strategy, the teacher divides the class heterogeneously
...groups of four (two students for each point of view). Then he or she
...ributes activity sheets for each opposing side so that the students can
...iliarize themselves with the point of view they are to be arguing. Groups
...eive different versions of the activity sheets to suit their reading levels.
...e easier version for each point of view may have more photographs or
...als to support the text than the more challenging versions. Then students
...asked to annotate their activity sheets with markings. They highlight
...portant key words, place a question mark next to a word or phrase that
...y don't understand, and place an exclamation mark next to ideas that they
...e passionate about.

...Next, the teacher jigsaws all of the students in the class so that each new
...oup discusses the same activity sheet. This helps to clarify the text and
...akes each student an expert in what they read. When they return to their
...riginal groups, they share their perspective with their partner who represents
...e same point of view. This is called flexogeneous grouping—groups are
...eterogeneous to start, homogeneous for clarification, and then they return
...their original heterogeneous group.

...Next, students decide how they are going to find primary source documents
...r visuals that will support their point of view. Will they make a chart or a
...raph? Will they find a picture or video? Will they draw an illustration? Will
...hey write a song or play a melody that was actually written during the time
...eriod? In other words, they construct their own or use an actual primary
...source document.

For primary students, use the following questionnaire (Figure 2.1). The answer key is as follows:

Row 1—Verbal/Linguistic Intelligence

Row 2—Logical/Mathematical Intelligence

Row 3—Rhythmic/Musical Intelligence

Row 4—Visual/Spatial Intelligence

Row 5—Bodily/Kinesthetic Intelligence

Row 6—Interpersonal Intelligence

Row 7—Intrapersonal Intelligence

Figure 2.1 Multiple Intelligences Inventory

Multiple Intelligences Inventory

Directions: Read each box. Color the ones that tell what you like.

I like . . .

writing stories	telling stories	reading	spelling	doing searches
math problems	counting	playing checkers	measuring things	making graphs
playing instruments	humming tunes	writing songs	listening to music	singing
puzzles	drawing	painting	making sculptures	looking at maps
playing sports	hiking	acting	moving around	dancing
playing games	group work	being the leader	talking to people	talking on the phone
keeping a journal	setting goals	thinking	time alone	reading alone
the outdoors	learing about weather	nature	animals	watching animals

(Adapted from Conklin 2004)

Challenging All Students

Curriculum that engages by providing students with challenges produces optimal opportunities for learning (Vygotsky 1978). Challenging work can take students slightly beyond their comfort zones, but that doesn't mean that it has to be difficult and stressful. When presented with challenging work, students know they have some of the tools to be successful. It does not mean that a student is completely a fish out of water, but he or she may need more tools to accomplish the work. This could mean that they have to research the topic, analyze a new diagram, consult with others, or ask good questions to find out more. Grappling with something that is not easy puts us out of our comfort zones just a little bit, but struggling is a necessary part of learning (Zmuda 2008). Knowledge and meaning are constructed when students struggle to make sense of a problem.

This idea of challenging students is synonymous with Vygotsky's zone of proximal development (1978). The zone of proximal development is "the distance between the actual developmental level as determined by independent problem solving and the level of potential development as determined through problem solving under adult guidance, or in collaboration with more capable peers" (Vygotsky 1978, 86). *Proximal* means "next," as in stretching learners to the next level of understanding. For many students to reach this next level, differentiation or scaffolding must occur (see Figure 2.2).

Figure 2.2 Zone of Proximal Development Diagram

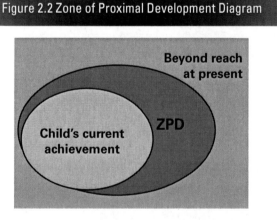

(Adapted from Vygotsky 1978)

Differentiation for All Students

While active learning reaches many learning st for various reasons, some students still struggle or of reading, writing, and speaking. When there active learning strategy lesson, struggling readers to be successful. Struggling writers will need diffe write something, and language learners will need di communicate effectively during discussions. At the o a text might be too easy for a gifted reader. Adva greater depth and sophisticated vocabulary, and th often not advanced enough for them in grade-leveled

The idea of differentiation is to make the conten while at the same time positioning the content at learning, so they will grow. When curriculum is positi have the chance to enter what psychologist Mihaly *flow* (1996). Flow can be defined as the state of min state of experience, that students feel when they are to they are doing. Flow can happen when they engage in a task. If a task is too difficult, students feel stressed and a hand, if a task is too easy, students become bored. The tasks that provide the right amount of challenge for stud

Figure 2.3 Learning Flow Diagram

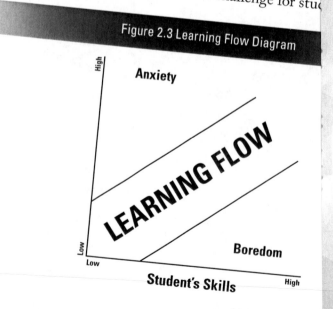

(Adapted from Csik

Finally, both pairs of students, being fully prepared, come together to iron out and negotiate a deal. For more information, please refer to the Negotiation strategy in this book.

So, how is this active learning strategy differentiated?

A differentiated lesson for Identity Crisis might look like this:

- Activity sheets were written at different levels so students would be comfortably challenged according to their readiness levels

- Students marked and annotated the text according to their unique interpretations and in a way that would support their comprehension of the text

- Students had two different groupings throughout the activity, making the environment "flexible" and appropriately challenging for all

- Students needed to support the content in some way with a video, a picture, song, poem, chart, graph, etc., allowing for differentiation through choice and learning preferences

- Cooperative groups would negotiate a deal that would be different from another cooperative group when their final products are presented to the class

The right way to differentiate materials is to consider what is right for your students. What will give them the right amount of challenge and still enable them to complete the task? The teacher-coach has to pre-assess his or her students to know what they need. Then, the teacher-coach can make thoughtful decisions concerning the curriculum, so all students can be appropriately challenged.

English Language Learners

Language learners come into our classroom environments with specific language needs. To communicate, they must be able to read, speak, understand, and write English. It makes sense that to support language development, these learners need opportunities for authentic language interaction.

Active learning offers the motivation for authentic communication so that language learners can produce and manipulate language (Fern, Anstrom, and Silcox 2005). The very nature of active learning strategies requires that students share their knowledge, question new knowledge, and consult together on what they know or have learned. This is more powerful for language development than mere rote language drills.

For language learners, the first step is understanding the language, but classroom activities should also naturally push students toward better language acquisition. According to Herrell and Jordan (2004), it is not just important for these learners to understand the content. They must also realize when others do not understand what they are saying. This moves the learner from just listening for understanding to practicing the formulation of words and sentences so they can communicate more effectively with others. Active learning includes the full circle of communication in which students both understand others and communicate with others. In effect, it helps them grow their language skills.

To support language learners in an active learning environment, teacher-coaches must make certain modifications. The environment must be a safe place where these students can take risks while learning the language. These learners will make mistakes as they communicate, but these mistakes should be welcomed as students seek to communicate. Instead of sitting in silence, they need to feel that they can ask for clarification. The teacher-coach sets the tone in every classroom by how he or she responds and models what is expected by the other students in how they treat the ELL student. Language-proficient students should be coached on when and how it is appropriate to help their ELL counterparts when they struggle with an idea or concept. A nurturing environment produced by the entire class will reduce student anxiety and gently guide them in the proper behaviors for school. Above all, teacher-coaches must be skilled at teaching content and language simultaneously (Fern, Anstrom, and Silcox 2005).

For primary students, use the following questionnaire (Figure 2.1). The answer key is as follows:

Row 1—Verbal/Linguistic Intelligence

Row 2—Logical/Mathematical Intelligence

Row 3—Rhythmic/Musical Intelligence

Row 4—Visual/Spatial Intelligence

Row 5—Bodily/Kinesthetic Intelligence

Row 6—Interpersonal Intelligence

Row 7—Intrapersonal Intelligence

Figure 2.1 Multiple Intelligences Inventory

Multiple Intelligences Inventory

Directions: Read each box. Color the ones that tell what you like.

I like . . .

writing stories	telling stories	reading	spelling	doing searches
math problems	counting	playing checkers	measuring things	making graphs
playing instruments	humming tunes	writing songs	listening to music	singing
puzzles	drawing	painting	making sculptures	looking at maps
playing sports	hiking	acting	moving around	dancing
playing games	group work	being the leader	talking to people	talking on the phone
keeping a journal	setting goals	thinking	time alone	reading alone
the outdoors	learing about weather	nature	animals	watching animals

(Adapted from Conklin 2004)

Challenging All Students

Curriculum that engages by providing students with challenges produces optimal opportunities for learning (Vygotsky 1978). Challenging work can take students slightly beyond their comfort zones, but that doesn't mean that it has to be difficult and stressful. When presented with challenging work, students know they have some of the tools to be successful. It does not mean that a student is completely a fish out of water, but he or she may need more tools to accomplish the work. This could mean that they have to research the topic, analyze a new diagram, consult with others, or ask good questions to find out more. Grappling with something that is not easy puts us out of our comfort zones just a little bit, but struggling is a necessary part of learning (Zmuda 2008). Knowledge and meaning are constructed when students struggle to make sense of a problem.

This idea of challenging students is synonymous with Vygotsky's zone of proximal development (1978). The zone of proximal development is "the distance between the actual developmental level as determined by independent problem solving and the level of potential development as determined through problem solving under adult guidance, or in collaboration with more capable peers" (Vygotsky 1978, 86). *Proximal* means "next," as in stretching learners to the next level of understanding. For many students to reach this next level, differentiation or scaffolding must occur (see Figure 2.2).

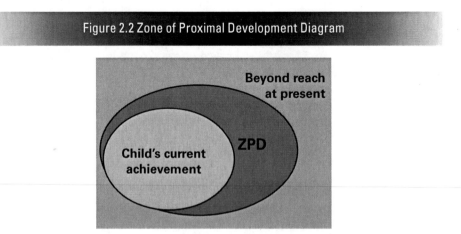

Figure 2.2 Zone of Proximal Development Diagram

(Adapted from Vygotsky 1978)

Differentiation for All Students

While active learning reaches many learning styles and types of learners, for various reasons, some students still struggle or lose interest with the tasks of reading, writing, and speaking. When there is text to read during an active learning strategy lesson, struggling readers will need differentiation to be successful. Struggling writers will need differentiation when asked to write something, and language learners will need differentiation to be able to communicate effectively during discussions. At the other end of the spectrum, a text might be too easy for a gifted reader. Advanced learners often seek greater depth and sophisticated vocabulary, and the level of complexity is often not advanced enough for them in grade-leveled texts.

The idea of differentiation is to make the content accessible to students while at the same time positioning the content at the cusp of students' learning, so they will grow. When curriculum is positioned this way, students have the chance to enter what psychologist Mihaly Csikszentmihalyi calls *flow* (1996). Flow can be defined as the state of mind (see Figure 2.3), or state of experience, that students feel when they are totally involved in what they are doing. Flow can happen when they engage in a difficult, yet possible, task. If a task is too difficult, students feel stressed and anxious. On the other hand, if a task is too easy, students become bored. The key is to orchestrate tasks that provide the right amount of challenge for students.

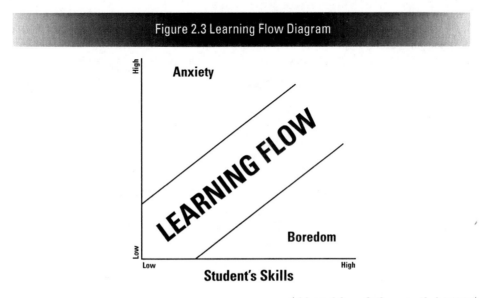

Figure 2.3 Learning Flow Diagram

(Adapted from Csikszentmihalyi 1996)

At times, some students need support or differentiation, so they can participate fully in an activity. Differentiating the process by which students participate becomes necessary, so all students can benefit from active learning. Let's examine the Negotiations and Settlements strategy. In this forum, students work in cooperative groups. Two students representing one point of view try to negotiate a settlement with two other students representing a different point of view. This can be done in science, for example, where pairs can discuss the use of genetic testing to diagnose cancer. While reading a book in language arts, pairs can represent characters with differing opinions who are asked to come to terms with their differences.

To begin this strategy, the teacher divides the class heterogeneously into groups of four (two students for each point of view). Then he or she distributes activity sheets for each opposing side so that the students can familiarize themselves with the point of view they are to be arguing. Groups receive different versions of the activity sheets to suit their reading levels. The easier version for each point of view may have more photographs or visuals to support the text than the more challenging versions. Then students are asked to annotate their activity sheets with markings. They highlight important key words, place a question mark next to a word or phrase that they don't understand, and place an exclamation mark next to ideas that they are passionate about.

Next, the teacher jigsaws all of the students in the class so that each new group discusses the same activity sheet. This helps to clarify the text and makes each student an expert in what they read. When they return to their original groups, they share their perspective with their partner who represents the same point of view. This is called flexogeneous grouping—groups are heterogeneous to start, homogeneous for clarification, and then they return to their original heterogeneous group.

Next, students decide how they are going to find primary source documents or visuals that will support their point of view. Will they make a chart or a graph? Will they find a picture or video? Will they draw an illustration? Will they write a song or play a melody that was actually written during the time period? In other words, they construct their own or use an actual primary source document.

Finally, both pairs of students, being fully prepared, come together to iron out and negotiate a deal. For more information, please refer to the Negotiation strategy in this book.

So, how is this active learning strategy differentiated?

A differentiated lesson for Identity Crisis might look like this:

- Activity sheets were written at different levels so students would be comfortably challenged according to their readiness levels

- Students marked and annotated the text according to their unique interpretations and in a way that would support their comprehension of the text

- Students had two different groupings throughout the activity, making the environment "flexible" and appropriately challenging for all

- Students needed to support the content in some way with a video, a picture, song, poem, chart, graph, etc., allowing for differentiation through choice and learning preferences

- Cooperative groups would negotiate a deal that would be different from another cooperative group when their final products are presented to the class

The right way to differentiate materials is to consider what is right for your students. What will give them the right amount of challenge and still enable them to complete the task? The teacher-coach has to pre-assess his or her students to know what they need. Then, the teacher-coach can make thoughtful decisions concerning the curriculum, so all students can be appropriately challenged.

English Language Learners

Language learners come into our classroom environments with specific language needs. To communicate, they must be able to read, speak, understand, and write English. It makes sense that to support language development, these learners need opportunities for authentic language interaction.

Active learning offers the motivation for authentic communication so that language learners can produce and manipulate language (Fern, Anstrom, and Silcox 2005). The very nature of active learning strategies requires that students share their knowledge, question new knowledge, and consult together on what they know or have learned. This is more powerful for language development than mere rote language drills.

For language learners, the first step is understanding the language, but classroom activities should also naturally push students toward better language acquisition. According to Herrell and Jordan (2004), it is not just important for these learners to understand the content. They must also realize when others do not understand what they are saying. This moves the learner from just listening for understanding to practicing the formulation of words and sentences so they can communicate more effectively with others. Active learning includes the full circle of communication in which students both understand others and communicate with others. In effect, it helps them grow their language skills.

To support language learners in an active learning environment, teacher-coaches must make certain modifications. The environment must be a safe place where these students can take risks while learning the language. These learners will make mistakes as they communicate, but these mistakes should be welcomed as students seek to communicate. Instead of sitting in silence, they need to feel that they can ask for clarification. The teacher-coach sets the tone in every classroom by how he or she responds and models what is expected by the other students in how they treat the ELL student. Language-proficient students should be coached on when and how it is appropriate to help their ELL counterparts when they struggle with an idea or concept. A nurturing environment produced by the entire class will reduce student anxiety and gently guide them in the proper behaviors for school. Above all, teacher-coaches must be skilled at teaching content and language simultaneously (Fern, Anstrom, and Silcox 2005).

Students with Special Needs

Active learning is ideal for inclusive classrooms. Studies show that students with disabilities excel when these strategies are used (Peterson, Feathers, and Beloin 1997). These strategies have already become a staple in many programs that work with students with special needs because of their success.

Because active learning takes into account the diverse learning styles of all students, those with disabilities naturally benefit from these strategies (Udvari-Solner and Kluth 2008). Studies show that students with disabilities grasp concepts with greater depth when they actively participate in the learning process (Richards 2008). Active learning strategies require that students participate fully with mind and body. While this benefits all students, it is absolutely necessary for students with special needs.

Many students with special needs have difficulty transferring classroom-learned skills to real-life contexts. By their very nature, active learning strategies help students make these difficult connections. Many of these strategies give real-life scenarios where conversations occur or viewpoints must be defended. Developing these real-life skills will put students ahead of the competition as young adults.

Conclusion

Active learning benefits all students for different reasons and in different ways. These strategies help special-needs students transfer classroom skills to real-life contexts because they have the opportunities to make those difficult connections through kinesthetic experiences.

The strategies presented in this book support varied learning styles so that all students can be led to capitalize on their strengths. Teacher-coaches can design lessons that focus on certain learning styles to reach more students depending on their particular strengths. Active learning supports higher-order thinking through challenging students with rigorous content. Differentiation can be used to help all students to be able to take on the challenging curriculum so they will grow. Finally, English language learners gain the language development they need through the myriad of discussions and questioning techniques used in an active learning classroom. The active aspects of the strategies help reach these students who are ever increasingly expanding their academic vocabulary through various learning experiences.

Let's Think and Discuss

1. Explain in detail some of your students' learning styles.

2. In what ways might an active learning strategy need to be differentiated for your students?

3. If you have English language learners in your classroom, explain specifically what kinds of modifications you will need to make to implement some of your favorite active learning strategies found in this book.

Chapter

Effective Grouping for Active Learning

Contrary to popular belief, not every active learning activity requires that students work in groups. Many of the strategies in this book call for students to work individually or in pairs to establish autonomy and actively practice the content—both necessary things for learning (Anderson, Reder, and Simon 1997). However, we do know that grouping is beneficial for students. Research states that groups should be used *at least* once a week (Lou et al. 1996). However, we recommend that paired learning or grouping be done daily.

The active learning strategies that do implement grouping use them primarily for discussions and projects. The discussion strategies demand that students work with others as they discuss opposing viewpoints, brainstorm ideas, and find meaning in texts. The project-driven strategies have students preparing for debates, presentations, or skits, among other things. For the latter, the work has to be both shared and divided up among group members. In light of these things, the ultimate goals for grouping during active learning are twofold: to help students develop productive discussions and to divide up work equitably among group members.

First, we will examine the rationale for using groups and why it benefits our students. Second, we will look at tips for ensuring productive discussions. Next, we will explore why variety is the key for helping students work effectively on group projects. Since students don't naturally work well in groups, we will consider ways to train students to work productively with others. Finally, we will look at tips for managing the nitty-gritty of group work.

To get students used to "talking content" with one another, a simple exercise can be used with index cards. Pose an open-ended question. Ask each student to respond on an index card and sign his or her name. Request that all students get out of their seats and find a partner. Each person shares their thoughts written on the index card with each other. Afterwards, they can discuss what was said. After two minutes, they exchange cards. They find a new partner and share their peer's idea written on the index card. Repeat the process three times.

The Rationale for Using Groups

Grouping students in the classroom can be tricky. Battling student personalities, potentially poor work habits among students, and the lack of student productivity can weigh heavily on the minds of teacher-coaches—much so that some teacher-coaches understandably decide it is not worth the hassle. Grouping can be hard work for *everyone*. But there are some good reasons to work through the "hard stuff" of grouping.

1. Yeah, I'm the expert!

When students work in groups, they have the opportunity to showcase their talents or expertise in a particular knowledge area. This, in turn, boosts students' self esteem when they can share something important. This particularly applies to students who struggle academically in school. These students need the experience of being the expert, having thoughtful insight, and offering an unknown talent every now and then. For example, a struggling reader might have the distinct ability to illustrate and help his or her group with a graphic novel. Another student might know filming and editing to help his or her group produce a YouTube™ video. There might be a rapper in the group who can put the words written by another group member to a great beat. Active learning offers avenues by which unknown talent can be tapped and shared. Grouping allows for differentiation of tapping into students' strengths.

2. Getting ready for the future!

Students need to learn to work with others because many workplace environments demand it. Grouping during active learning activities reflects how science is practiced in the real world using research teams. Businesses often hold brainstorming sessions to come up with new ideas for products. A restaurant staff has to work together to produce a lovely evening for a couple as they make sure they are seated, offered the specials, and served the food that the cooks prepared. Construction crews have to work together if they want the building to go up safely and according to deadlines. In all these examples, everyone's job is equally important, and everyone must pull his or her own weight for the group to be successful. The goal is the same for active learning strategies.

3. Let me do it!

Students need to learn problem-solving skills, and working with others provides those opportunities. This includes not only grappling with the problem presented in the lesson but also the problems that can come when working with others. Teacher-coaches can't expect students to know how to deal with these situations naturally. Leaving students to themselves can produce disastrous results. But with the right guidance and coaching, such as the GOPER model, students can learn to be successful in both of these situations and, in turn, become better problem solvers for life.

4. What? The world doesn't revolve around me?

Students need to understand that others have contributions and viewpoints that can be helpful. Often, students who prefer to work alone have trouble in groups because they feel their ideas are the best ones. Sometimes, these ideas might be the best ones. But often, they can learn from other ideas and even mesh the two together to have even better ideas. Learning to be open to other viewpoints is the goal of many active learning strategies, including Lobbyist Hearings, Stix Discussions, and Magnetic Debates.

5. My friend can teach me!

Collaborating with peers can offer plenty of unique opportunities for learning. A teacher-coach might explain a new concept to students, but have pairs discuss it afterwards. This allows students to personally refine it and incorporate it into their own understanding. On the other hand, allowing students to partner and conduct a think-pair-share periodically through that lesson or a carousel brainstorm in a small group might open up students' understanding when peers step in and explain. In fact, according to Marzano,

Pickering, and Pollock (2001), grouping students has a powerful effect on learning.

Overall, grouping students for active learning offers so many teachable moments. Watch any reality television show where people have to work together, and you quickly see conflict. The adults on those shows often don't know how to work collaboratively and have overall poor communication skills. While many of us may enjoy this form of entertainment, none of us want to see our students in these same situations in real life. Rather, we want our students to become effective collaborators, polish their verbal communication skills, and learn how to negotiate, persuade, and get along with others. Learning how to work effectively in groups for discussions and for projects will allow students to develop these desirable skills.

Tips for Productive Discussions

The goals of discussions are to brainstorm ideas, evaluate information, draw conclusions, and form opinions based on the information given. Students need smartly-crafted questions to use during a discussion. These types of questions should be open-ended and higher-order. Students will also need to know the differences between fact and opinion statements, in order for discussions to be successful in producing critical thinking. To prepare students, fact and opinion identification exercises can be practiced using statements from the newspaper, radio, television news, shows, and commercials.

During discussions, students will disagree. Students won't naturally know how to express their differences of opinions. As the teacher-coach, you can model the proper way to disagree during a discussion and have students practice disagreeing in their groups.

Language learners need to be dispersed throughout groups in the class, in order for them to have ample opportunities to use their language skills. All students need good modeling, so always model for the entire class with a good question and answer before assigning groups to discuss. Also, make sure the other students in the groups are prepared to be patient, respectful, and helpful when necessary. Often, it only takes pulling these other students aside and reminding them of what you want accomplished in their groups and of your expectations when language learners are present.

When grouping students, you may want to place talkative students together in one group and quiet students in another group. This will force both types of groups to discuss instead of allowing one student to dominate a group or all of them to not participate at all as outlined in the Differentiation section.

Variety Is the Key for Group Projects

Most often, teacher-coaches form groups for projects consisting of students at different ability levels. They do this because they believe it to be the egalitarian way. Other teacher-coaches only group students by ability, and in the process, certain students feel stigmatized. There are those who allow students to form groups of their own choosing and those who change the groups for each and every project. Consistently grouping students *only* one of these four ways can offer few benefits and bring many problems. One key to successful grouping is being flexible.

When asked, high-achieving students often prefer to work individually on projects because they feel that others, who they perceive don't work as hard or have less ability, will compromise their work. Struggling students can often feel intimidated and may not do work for fear that it won't be good enough. High-ability students might reaffirm these fears in how they respond. This scenario seems to undermine the whole goal of getting students to equally contribute to projects while at the same time learning to problem solve with one another.

Heterogeneous grouping can be a productive way to arrange students. Some studies among college students report that mixing students according to their ability groups shows improvement in all students' learning (Ballantine and Larres 2007). There are times when high-achieving students are needed to model higher-order thinking and strong, creative problem-solving skills. Their good model has the potential to help other students push themselves academically. However, depending on the age and maturity of students, this may not work well in every classroom. The problems tend to arise when there is too large an academic gap between your above-grade-level and below-grade-level students. In these instances, a teacher-coach will need to closely monitor groups to make sure that all students are contributing as equally as possible without intimidation or hurt feelings. Once again, please refer to the Differentiation section as a good example for strengthening students' self-esteem at every academic level.

Another great method is to use "seasonal partners." In the beginning of the year, each student receives a sheet and fills in a partner for spring, one for summer, one for fall, and one for winter. A partner from one season may be on the same academic readiness level, whereas another may be either higher or lower. Yet another may have a shared interest, and the last may be someone either whom they don't know or who is a favorite peer of theirs. The teacher-coach calls out to students, "Please find your fall partner." Students look at their charts in their notebooks, and without discussion, they quickly find their partners. This method can be used for a month, a term, or an entire year.

Give students an opportunity to choose their groups, too. This method works well because students enjoy working with their friends, and they know they can trust them. Friends don't feel shy about reminding everyone to carry their weight of the project, and each student feels the pressure to not let his or her friends down. A teacher-coach can switch this up by asking everyone to select new group members for the next project. This forces students to look for others with whom they can work.

An easier and possibly more productive way to heterogeneously group students is to place the highest level of students with on-grade-level students. Be sure there are at least two above-grade-level students (instead of just one student) in a group so that they can share responsibility. Then, group other on-grade-level students with your below-grade-level students. Both of these heterogeneous groups can more easily challenge one another to do their personal bests while not intimidating one another to the point of apathy.

Proponents of homogeneous groups like this grouping strategy because students don't have to worry about academic intimidation. Students on the same readiness levels have the potential to push one another to do one's personal best. At times, high-achieving students need to be pushed and challenged by others close to their academic abilities to make them sharper.

This works for the other groups, too. Homogeneous groups can free the teacher-coach to pay more attention and work more closely with struggling groups, whether they are gifted or below average. Students who are performing below average may need help on understanding content whereas gifted students may need help analyzing the content. There are many professionals who give more attention to one group at the expense of another. The caution is overusing homogeneous groups because it can cause some students to feel stigmatized and lose confidence in their abilities to work independently. To keep this from happening, be sure to switch up the groups often and try heterogeneous grouping and student-selected grouping. Homogeneous grouping should only be used when the reading selections or assignment can be tiered for students' academic readiness. Therefore, they are an advocate of flexogeneous grouping, as outlined in the differentiation section.

Another grouping strategy is called *flexogeneous groups* (Stix 2000). In this strategy, students are grouped homogeneously to start an activity. They are assigned the activity, and everyone in the group becomes an expert on the topic (e.g., identifying the central theme in a piece of text, reviewing the main character's development through the text). Once each group has become an expert on their respective topics, the groups are jigsawed to become heterogeneous, including at least one member from each of the original groups. The new groups are then provided an activity where each member of the group can contribute to the activity based on his or her original expertise (e.g., completing a report on the selected piece of text).

The most important thing to remember is to offer a variety of ways to group students (Kagan 1994). Switch groups often enough so that students don't become bored with one another, but also keep groups together long enough so they can learn how to resolve conflicts together.

Train Students for Group Work

For groups to be successful, students have to be taught how to work in groups. Working productively with others is not something that comes easily for everyone. For many of us, it is quite the opposite: a struggle. We have to learn to listen to others, wait our turn, and at times, compromise. Teaching these skills to our students will take time and patience. Many of the coaching strategies do just that.

First, students need to understand how to communicate effectively. For example, when a disagreement or misunderstanding occurs, have students state the facts, explain their viewpoint, and then listen to the other viewpoint. To achieve this, teacher-coaches can have certain students model this method for the class. Everyone can then participate in mock disagreements to practice these helpful behaviors. A good coaching strategy uses this model: Listen, Paraphrase, Respond. If a student first listens without interruption, then paraphrases what was just heard, the other student feels acknowledged. Then the student can bring up the point of disagreement. If students practice this strategy, they will become better collaborators.

Understanding how to collaborate will be difficult for some students who naturally prefer to work alone. One way to keep all students equally engaged is to assign student jobs or responsibilities to group members. These jobs should be meaningful and be equal in the amount of work required. At times, you can assign these roles to particular students, and other times, students can self select their roles within their groups. If students are assigned these roles, they can become the leader of the role and can have other students help them with the role. The roles can also be rotated so that all students have each role at some point.

Consider the following roles for a discussion:

Facilitator—This student is responsible for asking questions and keeping the discussion going so that the group can finish within a certain time frame.

Summarizer—This student summarizes what has been said after each question. The other students must approve this summary before going on.

Reflector—This student looks for opportunities to use their own wording to clarify points that each speaker is making.

Elaborator—This student looks for ways to connect the discussion to previous topics or class content.

Roles for group projects can be divided equally by content if applicable. For example, a social studies project might need perspectives on economics, government, history, and geography. Each student can take one of these responsibilities and finish the work for his or her group. For a science experiment, the roles might be the data recorder, material gatherer, and experiment performer. In this next example, all student members are in charge of a contribution and must provide text to explain their selections.

Consider the following roles for that project:

Illustrator—This student is in charge of drawing an illustration for the project.

Internet Image Collector—This student is in charge of downloading an image for the project, making sure not to violate copyright laws and providing a reference for that image.

Animation Collector—This student is in charge of finding and providing an appropriate animated image for the project.

Photographer—This student is in charge of using a digital camera to take a picture for the project.

However, we want students to realize that even though they are in charge of a specific task, they may ask their peers for guidance and help. It's impossible for each role to be totally "equal" to the others. These types of roles also allow for students to work independently within a group structure. Therefore, we honor those students who like to work individually as well as those who like collaboration.

As previously outlined, try to select roles that are equally weighted, but not defined to only one student. Grouping works better when students have the flexibility to work independently or ask for help from their peers. These roles have equal responsibility and work loads. All students should contribute equally and valuably to the group. In intermediate grades and higher, students can sign contracts that outline the objective of the group work and expectations of each group member. This helps create accountability and responsibility among group members. Assure the groups that they will be graded using peer assessments, self-assessments, and teacher-coach assessments. Knowing this helps encourage all students to fulfill their roles in the groups. Students can submit their peer assessments anonymously, if necessary, to gain honest information.

Managing Groups

To help students get to know one another so that trust can be established, a teacher-coach can conduct some icebreaker and team-building activities. The active learning strategies in this book can be incorporated for these. For example, the Layered Ball Discussions strategy can be used with personal questions that ask about favorite foods, teams, and movies. Groups can set out on short scavenger hunts, build a paper sculpture that represents their group, and play two truths and a lie that allow the others to guess which is true about that person. All these types of activities speed up the process of students getting to know one another and building trust.

Teacher-coaches should provide enough support to help groups work independently. They should make sure that each group has enough supplies so that they don't have to share with other groups. Each group should have a copy of the instructions that outline what they need to do both as a group and individually. This information sheet should be specific so as to eliminate as many frivolous questions as possible.

Students also need to learn time management so that their projects are completed on time. For example, a teacher-coach can show students how to conduct daily group meetings to discuss what they have finished and what will be worked on the following day. At the beginning of class, the teacher-coach asks each group what their plan is for the day and has them give a brief report aloud at the end of the class. He or she can also walk around the groups at the end of the class with a checklist to make sure that all students have completed the right amount of work. The work that has not been finished can then go home as homework.

Most importantly, students need to put in place organizational systems that work for them. For example, there needs to be a place where they store their group work, be it a folder that stays with one responsible group member, a folder that all students carry, or a physical place in the classroom where the work can be placed. This will prevent students from losing their work.

Conclusion

There are many important reasons for using groups during classroom activities. Students learn that others have valid opinions, that they are able to problem-solve successfully, and that there are things they can learn from their peers. Rich discussions can erupt and deep learning can occur as a result of grouping students, but these successes don't come easily. Students need solid instruction to know how to work with others effectively. To be really successful, these groups need to be managed effectively. Simple tips to manage these groups and keep it all organized can ensure that students are learning.

Let's Think and Discuss

1. With regard to grouping, what has been your biggest success in the past?

2. In the past, what has been the largest obstacle for group work in your classroom?

3. Describe in detail the ideas in this chapter that will help your students successfully work in groups.

Strategies that Activate Prior Knowledge

Connections for students occur when they bridge what they already know with what they are learning. For many students, activating prior knowledge is a skill that they must learn. Mastering this skill helps students approach learning with a purpose because they become aware of what they know and do not know about the topic. They then work to construct meaning from the experience. As a result, students' knowledge base grows and expands.

The strategies presented in this chapter activate students' prior knowledge. While participating in these active strategies, students dig deeply into Piagetan cognitive structures called *schemata*. As they learn more about a topic, they accommodate or make changes in previously held knowledge, and their connections between schemata become more complex.

Active learning strategies that activate prior knowledge include:

Carousel Brainstorming

Carousel Brainstorming is designed to identify the collective thinking of a group by using open-ended questions. In small groups, students "carousel," or walk, from one question to another, brainstorming together to write the best new answer for each question.

Brainstorming is a method of thinking up new concepts, ideas, or solutions. The goal in brainstorming is to generate as many ideas as possible within a time frame. The more ideas that are generated, the better the chance of finding a satisfying answer. Brainstorming with others brings out creative ideas that might not have been evident if students had been working alone. Open-ended questions are needed for brainstorming because they offer opportunities for many answers and are exclusively dependent on the creativity of students' thinking. The end result is open, not closed, and facilitates higher-order thinking in students. Open-ended questions provoke a higher-level response from students and responses can be easily written. Some sentence stems for open-ended questions include:

- Explain in detail another idea for. . .

- Describe specifically how you could change . . .

- Compose a list of other ways this could be solved . . .

- Generate a list of alternatives to . . .

- For what reasons . . .

- In what ways could this person have responded . . .

- What motives did this person have, and what did he or she want to accomplish. . .

There are some students who will, at first, be resistant to open-ended questions, but this is not because they are unable to answer these questions. Rather, it is because they are afraid to think on their own. Years of looking for the one correct answer have brought this fear of failure and embarrassment of getting the "wrong" answer (Jackson 2009). It will take time for these students to be at ease with these types of questions. To help them, model how to answer these questions. Keep encouraging them to answer these questions. And most importantly, be patient with them.

How to Do It

Carousel Brainstorming can be set up in a variety of ways. The preferred way is to hang posters or large sheets of chart paper on the walls around the room. Each poster should have a different open-ended question or directive written on it.

For example in social studies, questions having to do with leadership and governing are great to use at election time. These open-ended questions and directives can include:

1. Generate a list of as many leaders as you can think of (in school, or on a local or national level).

2. In your opinion, who is the worst leader in history? Explain in detail your reasoning.

3. Describe in detail the kinds of life experiences a good leader should have.

4. Generate a list of the worst qualities a leader could have.

5. Explain in detail how much education a good leader needs.

6. Generate a list of the kinds of job experiences a good leader should have.

7. Describe specifically the number one quality a good leader should have.

Divide the students into small groups of three to five students. Give each group a different-colored marker. Each group walks to a poster, discusses the question, and brainstorms possible answers. When they decide on an answer as a group, one student writes it down on the poster. Give the groups a time limit at each poster, or allow students to take as much time as needed before moving on to the next poster. Each group writes as many responses as possible within a given time period on a poster. Then, the group carousels to the next poster and repeats the process but passes the marker to a different student within the group. This allows all students to be the scribe at some point. This time, students must read the responses written by the previous groups before they begin to write new ideas. They cannot copy an answer that is already written down. Students repeat this process until they have visited all the posters. Keep track of student answers by tracking the colored markers on each poster. For example, group one used the green marker, so you can evaluate student answers by following the green answers on each poster.

Another way to use Carousel Brainstorming is by placing open-ended questions on papers in different file folders. The file folder is placed with students sitting together in groups at tables or desks. Each group of students has a different-color marker. The students discuss the question and brainstorm possible answers. When they decide on an answer, one student uses the marker to write it down on an answer sheet inside the file folder. Give a signal (such as ringing a bell) when student groups must rotate to a new file folder. Students repeat this process until they have "visited" all the file folders. Keep track of student answers by tracking the colored markers in each file folder until all folders are rotated. Once students have a clear understanding of the task, you may wish to begin negotiable contracting of assessment so that students are familiar with the expected criteria.

Ideas for Assessment

Carousel Brainstorming can be used to gather information about what students already know, what needs to be taught, and what should be differentiated for students. A teacher-coach's checklist to keep track of student responses can be as simple as checking for a recorded answer or responding with a check mark. Teacher-coaches can also rate student understanding of the topic using the following criteria:

- Student shows no understanding of the topic (✓–).

- Student has a limited or narrow understanding of the topic (✓).

- Student displays a sound understanding of the topic (✓+).

- Student shows a broad understanding of the topic (✓++).

Before they embark on the task, the teacher-coach and students can negotiably contract what will be observed. Choices may include but are not limited to:

- Students listen to one another.

- Students have meaningful conversations.

- Students write legibly, so other students will be able to read the text.

The criteria above can help teacher-coaches authentically assess as they differentiate the curriculum for students. Those students who have a strong grasp of the content need more challenging work so that they can continue to grow in their knowledge. Students who show a limited understanding of the content are most likely ready for the lessons that are prepared for the topic. And those who show no understanding of the topic will need the content scaffolded at first so that they can gain the necessary ground to participate in the classroom discussions and activities.

Applying the Strategy

There are an endless number of topics that teacher-coaches can use with the Carousel Brainstorming strategy. For example, in mathematics, you can ask young students about number representations. As you write different numbers like 6, 10, 4, and 2 on posters around the room, have students carousel brainstorm to draw or write representations of those numbers on the posters. For the number 2, some students might draw two circles, write the word two, or draw a face with two eyes. To activate prior knowledge in science, use topics like biomes and ecosystems around the world with a different one on each poster. Students will need to write at least one thing they know about that biome or ecosystem. In language arts, open-ended questions could include questions about books or their characters and could also incorporate mini-writing assignments such as the following:

1. A catchy first sentence for a story

2. An unusual setting for a story with a sentence about what makes it unusual

3. A sentence that describes a character's face

Virtual Field Trip

Setting up a Virtual Field Trip provides students a way to learn about a topic online instead of leaving the classroom. The teacher-coach sets up a website or a wiki page with links that take students on an online learning adventure. Students use what they learn to create a project that they can display and present.

Today's students spend much of their time outside school connected to technology, so it makes sense to bring the venue that they find so engaging into classroom instruction. Studies show that the innovative use of technology in classrooms improves student learning (Wishart and Blease 1999). This is largely because the visual stimulation that technology provides has the potential to engage students who are not motivated by standard classroom instruction. In essence, we are better off teaching to these students' learning styles by using technology (Bryant and Hunton 2000).

School budget constraints or the sheer impossibility of traveling to some of these investigative places (take Mars, for example) make Virtual Field Trips ideal for classrooms today. Even if there are not many personal computers or laptops available for students, a teacher-coach can lead the entire class using one computer and a projector, interactive whiteboard, or a website and wiki pages can be established.

How to Do It

Begin by selecting a topic for students to research. Set up a website or a wiki page for the virtual field trip. The organization of this digital page should include an introduction that welcomes the students and gives them a sneak peek into the assignment, assignment details that tell students what they need to know, links to specific websites, and an assessment rubric or checklist that will assess student projects.

- **Introduction**—Welcome students to the virtual field trip. Your text should be conversational. Give students a sneak peek into the assignment.

- **Assignment Details**—Everything students need to know about the assignment should be written here. Put the expectations into an outline form or in a paragraph. This section should include links to specific resources such as websites, apps, music, activity sheets, articles, and magazines. By visiting these links, students will experience the virtual field trip without having to leave the classroom.

- **Assessment**—This section can include a link to a rubric or checklist that will assess student projects, or you can just explain how their projects will be graded. Negotiable contracting (see Chapter 1) can be used with the class so that students have a clear idea of how they will be assessed. This section should also tell the due date of the project. This assignment can take a few days or between two and four weeks to complete, depending on the complexity of the project, the class time allowed, and the amount of homework time expected. It can also include an invitation to a parent viewing night if you desire to do this. This is the concluding part of the web page.

Explain that students will be doing a research project about a specific topic. Tell students they will take a virtual field trip to find out more about this topic. Show the website or wiki page for the virtual field trip to the class, using a projector, interactive whiteboard, or computer screens. Review all the requirements and due dates for the activity so that students know what is expected. Students might need some time in class to work on this and some time at home for homework. On the final due date, have students present their projects, and both the teacher-coach and peers can engage in performance assessment using the negotiated criteria. Invite parents, other classes, and staff to hear these presentations.

Ideas for Assessment

Assessment for this strategy should be based on student projects. As much as possible, try to keep these rubrics objective so that all students can succeed if they follow its guidelines. Figure 4.1 is a generic rubric that can be used for different kinds of projects. Notice that it contains objective things like facts and vocabulary that students can include. The rubric criteria and point values should be determined using negotiable contracting. Students should have access to these rubrics before beginning their projects. If desired, add more details to rubrics to make them specific to the projects, such as eye contact while acting something out.

Figure 4.1 Sample Virtual Field Trip Project: Rubric

Name:			Due Date:
Novice	**Apprentice**	**Proficient**	**Distinguished**
Student project includes no key vocabulary terms.	Student project includes a couple of key vocabulary terms.	Student project includes a decent amount of vocabulary terms.	Student project includes many vocabulary terms.
Student project does not include any key facts.	Student project includes a couple of key facts.	Student project includes a decent amount of key facts.	Student project includes many key facts.
Student project shows no understanding of the content.	Student project shows a little amount of understanding of the content.	Student project shows a decent amount of understanding of the content.	Student project shows complete understanding of the content.
Total Points:			
Teacher Comments:			

Applying the Strategy

Virtual Field Trips can be created for any topic and most content areas. For example, a social studies class might take a virtual field trip to find out more about the Middle Ages. A science class might use Virtual Field Trips to understand how to dissect a frog. A math class might explore tessellations, and a language arts class can perfect students' writing and learn about famous authors' lives.

True or False Game

True or False Game is adapted from the Two Truths and a Lie strategy attributed to Linda Schwartz Green and Diane Casale-Giannola (2011). It is designed to help students analyze information and become good at discovering small mistakes. Teacher-coaches give three statements to students. Two statements are true, and one is false. Students must select the false statement and give reasons for their answers.

This strategy involves critical thinking and utilizes students' prior knowledge of topics. More than ever before, today's students are bombarded with information and advertisements that make claims, some of which are not true. Students who possess strong critical-thinking skills will be able to sift through these false claims. Practicing this strategy will strengthen these important skills in students.

How to Do It

To introduce students to this strategy, model it by writing three statements about the topic you are teaching. Two of these statements should be true. One of the statements should be false. Make the false statement very subtle. Only a small part of this statement needs to be false. Explain that the class will play a true or false game. Present the three written statements to students. Tell students that one of the three statements is false.

Have students work together to analyze the statements and come to their conclusions. Students should justify their answers by explaining why the statement is false. Reveal the false statement to students. This can be repeated as a whole-class activity in which students write the false statements together. Discuss how to make part of the statement true. This activity teaches students to look for the little details that can trick them on a test. Repeat this several times until you are certain that students understand how to form these types of subtle statements.

Have students work together in their small groups to create their own true and false statements. Students should write three sets of statements. For each set, two should be true and one should be false. Students can then trade papers and try to select the false statement while also giving their justification for it being false. Finally, provide a way for students to check their answers. If desired, negotiable contracting can be used with the class so that students have a clear idea of the expectations of the assignment.

Ideas for Assessment

Ask students to use the negotiable contracting of assessment. What would they be looking for in their students' behavior if they were the teacher? Choices may include but are not limited to:

- Listen and respond to one another.

- Edit their sentences to see if they are clearly written for others to read.

- Ask another group to test their sentences to make sure that they can offer it to the class.

Assess how well students pick up on true and false statements by using this performance assessment chart. Keep a simple checklist (Figure 4.2) that shows their progress. Then, use student-designed true and false questions to assess how well they understand the subtlety of these statements. Information on assessments will help you to know if you need to review this with students or apply it to quizzes on other topics in class so that students can continue practicing it. Either way, this is a good strategy to keep students on their toes as critical thinkers.

Figure 4.2 Sample True or False Game Checklist				
	Has difficulty with T/F statements	Struggles at times with T/F statements	Can pick up T/F statements	Can easily pick up T/F statements
Jamal F.			✓	
Shana G.		✓		
Grayson P.				✓
Cynthia H.				✓

Applying the Strategy

True or False Games can be used for any content area. The following science example shows two true statements and one false statement about microorganisms.

1. Lichen is a plant, not a microorganism.

2. Whales can grow large by eating microorganisms.

3. Some microorganisms can make their own food, and other microorganisms can eat them.

(Statement #1 is false in this example.)

Here is a math example:

1. If you can fold a shape in half and one half exactly covers the other half, then we can say that the shape is symmetrical and the fold line is the axis of symmetry.

2. Some shapes have several different axes of symmetry, some have only one, and many shapes are not symmetrical at all.

3. A rhombus has four lines of symmetry.

(In this example, statement #3 is false.)

In a language arts or social studies classroom, a teacher-coach can use these games for a book study, vocabulary, spelling, or text comprehension.

Concept Attainment

This brainstorming strategy is adapted from the idea of inductive thinking (Taba 1971). In it, students organize and reorganize information with the ultimate task of labeling categories. They begin to organize the data by seeing relationships between details in the information. In using this strategy, concepts are formed, clarified, and extended. Students must use prior knowledge for this strategy. It calls for a student-centered approach to learning and allows for openness and flexibility in thinking.

How to Do It Before the activity, consider the topic to be studied, and generate a list of ideas that students might come up with when asked what they know about the topic. After making the list, organize the ideas into specific categories under the general topic heading. For example, if students are asked to tell about the different kinds of rocks and how they are formed, the ideas may be grouped under three subheadings: *igneous*, *sedimentary*, and *metamorphic*. Once you have an idea of the major heading and subheadings of the topic to be discussed, the activity is ready to begin.

1. Place students into small groups. Present the topic to students and ask them to brainstorm everything they know about rocks. Each student shows what each knows about the topic. Then, allow students to share their ideas in their small groups.

2. Have students share their ideas aloud. Write their ideas on the board in an organized fashion without giving headings or titles to the grouped topics. The idea is that students determine how you are grouping these ideas and give the headers or titles to each group. Students should be encouraged to give subheadings within groups to extend their thinking.

3. Once students have completed the task, they should talk about what they observed by participating in this strategy. Some groups will dive much deeper into the process and create a detailed organizational tree, whereas other students will only reach the main subheading level of discussion.

Once the activity has been explained, and before implementation, use negotiable contracting of assessment so that students are aware of the parameters of the assignment.

Ideas for Assessment

Pay special attention to students who need reinforcement with this strategy, and pull them aside for extra practice. One way to assess student thinking is to have them write short one-paragraph reflections as tickets-out-the-door. This reflection should be about what they observed while participating in this strategy. This can help you to know if students understand why certain concepts connect better than others. It can also provide better insight into how your students think or how students might have done it differently if given the chance.

Applying the Strategy

Concept Attainment can work with all content areas. In math, an example would be to ask students to write down everything they know about shapes and share their lists with others sitting nearby. Then, have a few students share their lists aloud. Students might say *corners, sides, vertices, edges, pyramids, flat, circle,* etc. As students read these characteristics, place them into three unnamed categories: two-dimensional, three-dimensional, and both. At the end of the discussion, see if students can name the three categories. In language arts, concept lists could be created around characteristics of book characters. The main categories could be protagonist and antagonist. In social studies, students could list what they know about the American Civil War. Categories could be agrarian society, economic differences, social differences, state vs. federal rights, and slavery.

Layered Ball Questions

For the Layered Ball Questions strategy, adapted from the Rainbow Ball strategy created by Linda Schwartz Green and Diane Casale-Giannola (2011), the teacher-coach writes a different question on colored sheets of paper and then crunches each paper into a ball, one on top of the other layer, until all the questions have been included and the ball is large. Students walk around and pass the layered ball, unwrapping a layer and answering the question on that layer.

As students work to answer the questions, they must use prior knowledge about that topic. Other students can chime in with their ideas and can add to that prior knowledge. This strategy takes the "boring" question-and-answer discussion format and makes it more interactive, adding in a level of mystery to see what question each student will get.

The Layered Ball Questions strategy helps students to focus their attention because of the movement involved. This enables students with attention problems or hyperactivity to focus and be engaged and, in turn, motivates students with attention issues (Kounin 1977). Students also work on their social skills with this strategy because they have to interact with others as they answer the questions found in the Layered Ball, thus promoting group interaction. It also provides students with the chance to see others model the right ways to approach and answer these questions as the ball is passed around and to practice that approach.

How to Do It

This strategy begins by selecting a handful of questions about a topic. The questions can be based on math facts, vocabulary, or a reading selection in any content area. They can be random questions or questions that build from one another, going from basic on the outside to more complex on the inside. Here are steps for the strategy:

1. Write a question on the middle of a sheet of colored paper.

2. Once the question is written, crunch the paper into a tight ball.

3. Then, write the next question on a different sheet of paper and crunch that question paper around the previous paper ball. The ball will be a little bit larger.

4. Repeat this process until all of the questions have been written and wrapped around the paper ball. Six questions are ideal.

5. If the questions build on one another, the most-complex question must be in the center of the ball and the least complex on the outer layer.

If this activity is completed in small groups, multiple layered balls will need to be created, one for each group. A student would then take off the outer layer of paper, read the question aloud, and then answer it. Then, the student passes the ball to another student within the group to do the same thing. This repeats until all the layers have been removed and the questions have been answered. If formal assessment of the student responses is desired, negotiable contracting (see Chapter 1) can be used so students are aware of the criteria for this activity such as listening and responding well to one another, and writing simple to complex sentences.

If you are the facilitator of the ball, then you can color-code the questions and toss them to the students who can answer the questions. For example, the green paper might be the most complex question, so you will toss the ball to a student who needs a more-challenging question. An example of this might be, "Based on the events in the story, give three character traits that describe Pricilla, and tell why you think that." This is a more difficult question because it is open-ended. We want the students to tell us those character traits. The red paper might be the easier question, so when the outer layer is red, toss the ball to a student who needs the support given on that sheet of paper. An example of an easier question could be, "In what ways is Pricilla the perfect and yet unexpected hero of this story? Support your answer with references to the text." This question is easier because we are telling the students that she is a perfect and unexpected hero. We want the students to tell us why.

Ideas for Assessment

Have students keep track of their answers and then report them to you. For example, if the strategy is used for true and false questions, have students place the true statements in a pile and the false statements in a different pile. If you used the same colors on all the balls, at a quick glance you can see the colors in each pile to know how students answered the questions. For example, the yellow and orange papers are true statements and the blue and green papers are false statements. You can also have students give you a show of hands to tell you if they got them all correct or who missed just one or two questions. Walk around the classroom assessing student performance based on the rubric bank in areas such as their ability to discuss and ask quality questions, and addressing key issues to answer the questions. Figure 4.3 shows a sample observation checklist that could be used with this strategy.

Figure 4.3 Sample Observation Checklist				
	Discusses quality questions	Provides clear and reasonable responses	Is respectful to others' responses	Follows directions of activity
Sophia	✓–	✓	✓	✓+
Rebecca	✓+	✓+	✓–	✓
Joel	✓	✓++	✓	✓+
Adrian	✓++	✓–	✓++	✓+
Adam	✓++	✓–	✓++	✓+
Elizabeth	✓	✓++	✓–	✓
Sam	✓+	✓	✓	✓–

Key	
✓–	no understanding
✓	limited understanding
✓+	sound understanding
✓++	broad understanding

Applying the Strategy

While this strategy can be used to foster higher-order thinking, it can also be used as a basic strategy that excites and gets students thinking about what they already know. For example, you can write various math facts on each layer and use this as a warm-up for the class. A fill-in-the-blank sentence can be written on each layer to review for an upcoming social studies quiz. Language arts students can unwrap vocabulary words they must use in complete sentences. Science students can review the periodic table by giving the element for a symbol.

Conclusion

It is important that students learn how to activate prior knowledge so that they can build upon that and construct new knowledge. The strategies in this chapter are ones that activate prior knowledge; they include Carousel Brainstorming, Virtual Field Trips, True or False Games, Concept Attainment, and Layered Ball Questions. Carousel Brainstorming allows students to "carousel," or walk, from one question to another, brainstorming together to write the best new answer for each question. Virtual Field Trips provide students a way to learn about any topic online and then create projects that they can display and present. True or False Games present two true statements and one false statement to students to give them practice analyzing information and honing their critical-thinking skills. Concept Attainment is a brainstorming strategy that has students organizing and reorganizing information with the ultimate task of labeling categories. For the Layered Ball Questions strategy, students take turns tossing a paper ball, unwrapping a layer, answering the question written on that layer, and then tossing it to a different student.

Let's Think and Discuss

1. Describe in detail which strategy in this chapter would be easiest for you to implement right away.

2. What are some possible topics your class could use for Carousel Brainstorming?

3. Look at the overall design for the year. Select four times you could use this activity, spreading the strategy out throughout the year.

Chapter

Discussion Strategies

Discussion strategies are valuable skills for every part of life. It is important for students to know how to communicate their thoughts effectively. The skill of persuasion is something that students can practice and hone. Most importantly, discussions bring out the diverse viewpoints that can help students make informed decisions and sometimes change their minds. The *Common Core State Standards* define this as being college and career ready. These standards dictate that students should be involved in rich, structured conversations in many venues. Students should not only contribute to these conversations (making comparisons, contrasts, analyzing, and synthesizing information) but also listen to what others say so that they can build upon these ideas as they seek to express their own, both clearly and persuasively (CCSS 2010).

The discussion strategies in this chapter include:

The first five strategies mentioned here are intended for upper elementary through high school, while the last five strategies mentioned are appropriate for all grades.

Lobbyist Hearing

During a Lobbyist Hearing, students take on the roles of lobbyists and represent four or more points of view. Students simulate participating in public meetings, in which members listen to the persuasive opinions of different interest groups to determine an important decision. These panel members can be students from the class, students from other classes, or adult volunteers. The student-interest groups argue and cajole, trying to persuade a panel to their point of view about what should be done. The panel can act as part of the judges, legislators, lawyers, or congressmen and congresswomen. It can be any setting you choose: a town meeting, a union hall, a political club, a congressional caucus, etc. The choices of a forum are endless, limited only by the imagination. Students enjoy this simulation because they can act out a part to the fullest, whether they represent someone they agree or disagree with in real life. This is fun for students because they can place themselves in roles they have never imagined before.

A Lobbyist Hearing is full of opportunities for discussion. The diverse viewpoints represented in this strategy help students to see that there is more than one way to look at a situation. It also provides an opportunity for students to go outside their comfort zones and represent a viewpoint that they may disagree with in a real situation. This helps students to empathize with other viewpoints, even if they do disagree, and it gives them practice in the art of persuasion.

How to Do It

First, decide on a controversial topic to be discussed. There should be at least four different viewpoints about this topic. These perspectives can be for or against, but they can also be perspectives that don't necessarily fall under that category. If it is a controversial issue where sides are apparent, be sure to have two pro and two con viewpoints. Assign students viewpoints for this activity. Many students will not agree with the viewpoints that they have been assigned in real life. Explain that it is important for students to stretch themselves to think about the issue from a different perspective and be able to defend and argue for it. Once the viewpoints are determined, write teaser and information sheets, gather research information for students to use, or be able to point students in the right direction for research on the viewpoints. Talk about techniques of persuasion with students so that they know how to persuade the panel to agree with their viewpoints.

Below are some criteria to be negotiably contracted with students to help them understand what it means to use persuasive techniques:

- The thesis is reasonably developed.
- Points are highlighted with ardor, and the approach gives off a strong energy level.
- The reader or listener can follow the argument or point of view to the extent that the thesis has been molded and developed and is held by vivid imagery.
- Written or spoken words are enthusiastic, dynamic, and vigorous.
- Written or spoken words show attachment to a cause through fervor and deep devotion.

After doing research, have students use the power of persuasion to write speeches on key points of their argument. The key points should be divided up so that each student's speech represents at least one key point for the Lobbyist Hearing. Negotiable contracting can be used with the class so that students are familiar with the expectations of the assignment. Provide a time limit (e.g., one to two minutes) for these speeches to make students more comfortable with writing them. On the day of the hearing, allow students to present their arguments. The panel then discusses the arguments and makes a decision.

Ideas for Assessment

One way to assess student understanding is through the content and performances of their speeches. Be sure to model good techniques for speeches so that students are prepared to give good presentations. You may use a point-based rubric like the following to assess these speeches. Point values can be determined during the negotiable contracting stage.

Figure 5.1 Lobbyist Hearing Speech Sample Rubric

Criteria	Points
Body included persuasive points, which are:	
Conclusion summed up the content	
Made eye contact	
Voice was loud enough to be heard and clearly articulated	
Introduction was engaging and thorough	
Used visual aids	
Total	

Applying the Strategy

For language arts class, a Lobbyist Hearing can be used to talk about banned books or controversial authors. Controversial science topics can include evolution, cloning, and stem cell research. Social studies topics include events from the past such as celebrating Columbus Day, erecting Civil War statues to honor the Confederate soldiers, current political debate topics, and immigration laws. Math topics may include geometric proofs or architectural designs.

Accountable Talk

The Accountable Talk strategy involves listening attentively to others. Students work as partners to evaluate each other's public discussion and presentation skills. This strategy can be used alongside of the Lobbyist Hearing, Stix Discussion, or any other strategy where we want students to assess each other on how well they speak.

Accountable Talk is an activity that increases the positive traits students possess to become good speakers, convincing negotiators, lobbyists, and skilled speech makers. Whereas a teaching strategy for primary grades would focus on the ability to understand and use the content proficiently, Accountable Talk is a strategy for secondary grades that involves listening attentively to others. This strategy focuses on the delivery of the content and students' behavior in a group setting. These are major concerns and top priorities of businesses, companies, and corporations hiring adults. By using Accountable Talk, teacher-coaches can help students achieve their goals.

How to Do It

To begin this strategy, partner students. Present a scenario to students that asks for their help in teaching something. This can be an advertisement (e.g., a museum needs docents to lead tours), a formal announcement (e.g., the principal announces a need for student teachers to teach a math concept to younger students), or a written invitation (e.g., guides are needed in the science lab to show a student audience how an experiment works). Have student partners prepare for the same presentation together. Then, on the day of the presentation, student A and a group from the class watch Student B present. Then Student A presents while Student B and a new group from the class watch him or her present. Students use an observation sheet with the following qualities to assess their counterpart during the activity.

Students should focus on the following as the active participant in the Accountable Talk:

- Actively speaks and participates
- Makes eye contact with others

- Refers to notes for important information

- Asks quality questions in a thoughtful manner that furthers conversation

- Responds to others

In the same manner, students should avoid the following behaviors:

- Speaks in a condescending way

- Interrupts another person

- Engages in conversation on the side

- Does not stay on topic

- Makes fun of others

The first student should present while the other student assesses. After a set amount of time (5 or 10 minutes), have students switch places and gather a new audience to participate in the presentation, and the other student now assesses his or her counterpart. Once the activity has been described in detail, you may wish to implement negotiable contracting of assessments. After the activity, allow partners to discuss how well they performed. In a positive fashion, students should comment on their strengths, and then discuss how they could improve on the areas of weakness. Consider modeling how to discuss the activity so that students use appropriate language and do not inadvertently offend anyone.

Ideas for Assessment

The peer assessment mentioned above is an integral part of this activity. It should provide the information a teacher-coach needs for each student. The teacher-coach should also be charting how well students are progressing based on the criteria for negotiable contracting of assessments. The activity sheet for an observational checklist might look like Figure 5.1.

The teacher-coach can also keep a similar chart for each student as well in order to complete an assessment of each student's performance and participation. See Figure 5.2 for a sample.

Figure 5.2 Accountable Talk: Performance Assessment

Name: _____

Accountable Talk Observation

Directions: Each time your partner does one of the following, place a check in the box.

Your partner's name _____

Positive

Actively speaks and participates:

Responds to others:

Refers to his or her notes or any text with pertinent information:

Makes eye contact with the person who is speaking or listening:

Asks quality questions:

Negative

Speaks in a condescending way:

Interrupts another person:

Engages in conversation on the side:

Does not stay on the topic:

Makes fun of others:

Figure 5.3 Sample Student Performance and Participation Chart

	Actively speaks and participates	Makes eye contact with others	Refers to notes for important information	Asks quality questions
Joseph	✓+	✓–	✓+	✓+
Samantha	✓–	✓+	✓	✓
Alice	✓+	✓–	✓	✓+
Courtney	✓–	✓+	✓–	✓+
Oscar	✓	✓+	✓+	✓
Olivia	✓+	✓	✓–	✓+
Steven	✓	✓–	✓+	✓

Key	
✓–	no understanding
✓	limited understanding
✓+	sound understanding
✓++	broad understanding

Describe in detail the two most interesting points your partner made and what made them stand out to you.

_____

_____

_____

Out of the things you have added to the discussion, describe specifically the one that is most important.

_____

_____

_____

Applying the Strategy

Accountable Talk can be used in any content area in the most basic way of teaching others through public speaking about the content that students are learning. For example, math students can use Accountable Talk to teach others in small groups about multiplying fractions. Accountable Talk can be used in language arts to teach others about genres or to present how-to speeches. Science teacher-coaches can use Accountable Talk to reinforce information on cells, allowing students to present to other classes or staff. Social studies classes can use Accountable Talk to present information on different cultures, famous people, or student-generated "museum pieces" to parents.

Magnetic Debate

The Magnetic Debate is a discussion strategy in which participants are given an opportunity to influence others through persuasive speeches, sincere advice, and education so an informed decision can be made on a controversial issue. Teacher-coaches make the selection of the area of study and have the students research the specific topic. Then, positions are assigned "for" or "against," with a portion of the class as "fence-sitters" or the "undecided" element who can be swayed one way or the other. Then, the students debate the issue.

More than any other strategy, the Magnetic Debate places students in the position of working on their abilities to persuade audiences. Students must combine top-notch research with finessed speaking skills so that others will want to side with their views. This strategy gives students practice empathizing with others as they prepare these types of speeches. It forces the students preparing and practicing the speeches to think like others would think so that they can become effective communicators. It also gives the students who are making the decisions during the debate opportunities to practice critical thinking. These students must analyze the facts and nuances set before them so that they can make informed decisions.

How to Do It

To begin, decide on a controversial issue to be discussed. The controversy should be broken down into subcategories that can be argued. Distribute activity sheets to give them background information. Write teaser sheets to engage the students about the controversial issue. These activity sheets place students as active participants in the controversy. Locate student-friendly information covering the different positions, so students will be able to research the necessary facts as an extension to the activity sheets. If desired, the activity sheets can serve this purpose, too. So that all students will be engaged in preparing and working toward the debate, divide the class into two groups. One half will prepare for the Pro position and the other half will prepare for the Con position. Within both of those positions, assign the subcategories of the topic so that *all* students spend time doing valuable research on the correct topics. Students should be partnered for the research. Have students on both sides of the issue cover each topic because each topic is subject to a rebuttal and followed by a persuasive speech from the opposing side. For example, if discussing the differences between political parties, sub categories would include state rights and political platforms.

Once students have had enough time to research adequately, have them write their rough drafts for the one- or two-minute speeches and allow student peers to edit the speeches for clarity. Allow students to use note cards to prompt their speeches and encourage them to use visuals like graphs, video clips, pictures, and other things during the debate. These special visuals will help them make their points persuasive to the audience.

On the day of the debate, select an odd number of students (3, 5, or 7) representing both sides to suddenly serve as "undecideds" or to sit on the interrogation committee. Tell them to forget all the things they have learned during their research thus far. These students will not give their speeches but rather serve as decision makers for the debate. Their partners will take over the speeches for the activity. These students should clear their minds of all opinions on the topic. Have students take notes or fill out graphic organizers during the debate to keep them engaged and actively learning. The same holds true for the interrogation committee, as they must clear their minds and become neutral. After each pair of students have debated, it is their role to ask questions for clarification.

To prepare the classroom, use masking tape to make a line on the floor down the center of the classroom. Students who speak for the Pro side will sit on one side of the classroom, and students who speak for the Con side will sit on the other side of the classroom. The "undecideds" will place their chairs directly over the line of tape and sit down. The interrogation committee sits at the head of the classroom. See Figure 5.4 for a sample seating diagram.

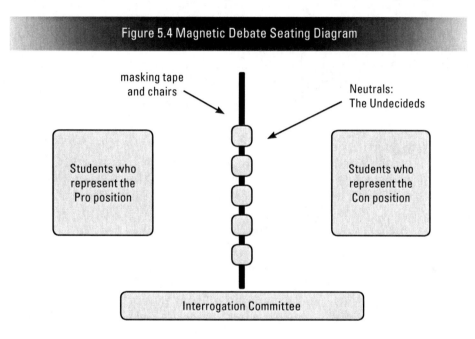

Figure 5.4 Magnetic Debate Seating Diagram

masking tape
and chairs

Neutrals:
The Undecideds

Students who
represent the
Pro position

Students who
represent the
Con position

Interrogation Committee

(Adapted from Stix and Hrbek 2002)

Set the stage by calling all participants involved in the simulation to order, and then state that a decision has to be made to determine a solution to their controversial issue. Call out the first category and begin with the Pro point of view. The person who is responsible for this item stands up and addresses the interrogation committee and the "undecideds." After the speech, allow the interrogation committee to ask one or two questions. This should be another subgroup. It should never be the teacher-coach. Working toward student-centeredness is key. Next, instruct the person responsible for this category from the Con perspective to give a short rebuttal to what has been said. After the speech, allow the interrogation committee to ask one or two follow-up questions.

After the category is completed, allow the "undecideds" to move their chairs about two feet closer to the group that has persuaded them. You may see the chair move in one direction for part of the class and then back in the other direction during the later part of the presentations. As the sides debate, instruct all students to write notes in their graphic organizers. Call the next category, but let the Con point of view begin, followed by the Pro point of view. Alternate for each turn.

After all categories have been heard, the side to which the largest number of "undecideds" has moved their chairs wins the debate. Once the activity has been described in detail to the students before its implementation, this would be a good time to use negotiable contracting of assessments.

Ideas for Assessment

Once the debate ends, have students reflect on it and the arguments they witnessed. This can be done in a class discussion, ticket-out-the-door, or a small-group discussion. The information you glean from students will tell you what they learned about the topic and the activity.

Applying the Strategy

Magnetic Debates can work well in a content area where a given topic has two over arching viewpoints. Social issues tend to work best, and they cover so many content areas. For example, social issues concerning science include organ donation, animal rights, and environmental protection. Social issues in social studies include child labor or sweatshops, famine, human rights, and welfare. Language arts topics can include library censorship or a debate about characters (e.g., Was the wolf really the bad guy in *The Three Little Pigs*?). In math, students can discuss what they believe is the best way to solve a math problem. Many of these topics can be simplified for young students. For example, have students debate the health of school lunches, getting a classroom pet, haircuts and hair color permitted for school, school uniforms, homework, and the classroom movie to be watched during a party.

Socratic Method

The Socratic Method is used primarily as a process of inductive questioning through small steps, with gaining knowledge about a topic as the goal. In a classroom, a teacher-coach can use a set of questions to provoke students to think about something. The questions push students to examine what they know with the result of them analyzing a topic in depth.

By using the Socratic Method, learners can come to value and recognize good questions while also improving upon a careful method of thinking. Students become more curious about the topic. They experience the joy of discovery. Students also get immediate feedback, and teacher-coaches can monitor student understanding by making adjustments, clarifying, and correcting misgivings immediately instead of waiting until the end of the unit test to find out that students did not understand the material. For the teacher-coach, instruction becomes more interesting because he or she can quickly glean the thought processes of the students. Classes will respond differently, so even content-area teacher-coaches who teach the same class multiple times daily will not grow bored with student responses. This method also allows teacher-coaches to see student potential, as some students might pose exceptional questions that might not happen during a regular class.

Some might mistakenly think that the Socratic Method requires very little preparation. On the contrary, to implement the Socratic Method in class, there is strategic teacher-coach preparation involved. First, teacher-coaches should make a list of good open-ended questions to ask and mentally rehearse the conversation beforehand. The first questions are designed to show what students understand about the topic so the teacher-coach knows where to begin. The questions need to follow a logical sequence of steps that takes learners from one point of knowledge to another. The questions should follow a logical path that supports what the teacher-coach wants students to learn. These questions should be specific enough to lead students to the desired understanding while also engaging students so that curiosity is piqued. If students answer incorrectly, a teacher-coach can pose a question that asks them to cite a reference, to explain more specifically, or to offer logic as to how they arrived at this answer. Not all questions will be the best or even appropriate, so teacher-coaches need to be open to the idea of fine-tuning how they question their students.

How to Do It

To begin, look for a topic that has more than one viewpoint within the objective you need to cover. Think of the final question or result you want students to reach. Then, work backward to design open-ended questions that progress and lead students to that desired result or end. There are four types of questions to choose from, as depicted in Figure 5.5.

Figure 5.5 CCSS Questions for the Socratic Method

Key Ideas and Details	• What are some of the unusual things you noticed about...? • What are you thinking about this? • For what reasons did the author say . . .? What did he mean by this? • What is the purpose of the text featured on these pages? • Describe in detail what conclusions you can make about. . . • What factors might change the information? Consider what you have read previously.
Vocabulary Acquisition and Use	• The phrase "_____" could mean _____ in this context. • What text evidence helps the reader understand the meaning of _____ on page _____? • Can you explain . . . ? • What is the correct way to define this? • How could this be said in your own words?
Craft and Structure	• In what ways is this text biased? • Explain in detail whose viewpoint is depicted in this text. • From what other perspectives can this be told? • In what ways does the author use the symbol of _____ in the text? Is this effective? Why or why not? • Do you think it is fair to _____? Why or why not? Use the text to support your claim! • Discuss specifically what you believe is the author's intended message in writing this text. Justify your thinking, using text evidence.
Integration of Knowledge and Ideas	• Explain specifically how we know that this document is important. • If this is true, what else could be true? • Describe in detail how this affects our lives. • How do you know that the author of _____ understood the _____? • What kinds of experiences would he have needed? • In what ways are these three texts the same? In what ways are they different? • In what ways does the poster tell us about the people and events during the time in which it was created? • Explain specifically how you can use the text and related texts to support the idea that _____. • How do you know this is true? Is it always true?

(Murphy and Conklin 2014; Adapted from Taba 1971 and Stix 2014)

Ideas for Assessment

During the activity, use a simple checklist to keep track of student participation in the discussion, which is an excellent use of performance assessment authentic to the task. Place a mark next to a student's name each time he or she speaks. Once you identify who is participating and who is not, steer the conversation toward the students who need to participate more and away from those who are overparticipating. This can be done by simply asking a student what he or she thinks about the last comment. Pull students aside who have a difficult time letting others participate, and gently talk to them about giving others a chance to talk. For example, you can explain that their contributions are highly valued and beneficial to the class, but ask them to not talk until the others have had a chance to speak. A sample assessment chart can be found in Figure 5.6. This chart can be modified to be used by either students to assess their peers or teacher-coaches to assess students. The criteria for assessment should be negotiably contracted ahead of time and center around displayed behaviors such as listening and responding, adding new information, and analyzing peer comments.

Figure 5.6 Sample Assessment Chart

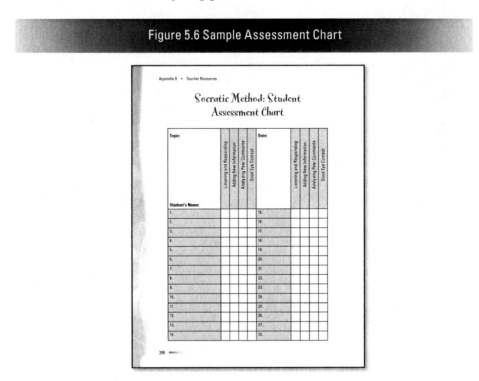

After the discussion, students can write a paragraph reflecting on the discussion. What students write can give you a strong indication of whether they are gleaning what you want them to as a result of the discussion. You can always have a follow-up discussion if students are not connecting to the topic or the content.

Applying the Strategy

Any of the topics already mentioned in this chapter would work well for Socratic Method discussions. Make sure that the questions are open-ended and can be seen from more than just one viewpoint. For language arts, hold Socratic discussions about poems, short stories, picture books, or novels. In math, instead of telling students the answer to a problem or even how to solve that math problem, ask students how they could approach solving the math problem by designing something, like a new playground. This requires students to think critically about the math before being told how to do it, which is more passive. In the same way, in a science class model an experiment for students and then ask them what just occurred in the experiment without explaining it first. When students offer an idea of what just occurred, steer the discussion to make them uncover what the experiment was used to demonstrate. In social studies, have students explore a leader's decisions, tracing back to the reason why certain events occurred in order to help them make meaning and connections.

Stix Discussion

The Stix Discussion (Stix 1999) is a discussion strategy that has four distinct viewpoints as well as an inner circle and an outer circle that equally participate in a discussion. This strategy is a modification of the inner-outer circle or fishbowl discussion. The students in the inner circle and the outer circle will change roles so that everyone gets an equal chance to participate.

This strategy takes discussions to a more complex level because there are four viewpoints that are argued (as opposed to just two different viewpoints in a regular discussion). All students are actively listening, so they can respond and contribute in one way or another to the discussion. Whether the students have the liberty to speak because they are inside the discussion circle or they are responding to the comments via written notes, everyone has a reason to listen critically.

How to Do It

To begin, divide the class into four points of view—two Pro and two Con—on any given controversial topic. What makes this strategy interesting is that all four viewpoints come together to discuss the topic.

1. Write or locate information guides that support each viewpoint and distribute these to students.

2. Give students time to talk about the information in their groups. Divide the main points that each of them will defend. Students should perform further research through web searches and extra reading. Information should be shared and discussed in their groups.

3. Jigsaw the groups so that each one has at least one member from all four viewpoints. Students should learn about the other perspectives in the new groups. This will help them create stronger positions for their own point of view.

On the day of the discussion, place one-third of the chairs in an inner circle. Behind each inner-circle chair, place a desk. Behind each desk, place two or three chairs. All chairs should be facing toward the center of the circle. This will create an inner circle and an outer circle. See Figure 5.7 for a sample seating diagram.

Figure 5.7 Stix Discussion Seating Diagram

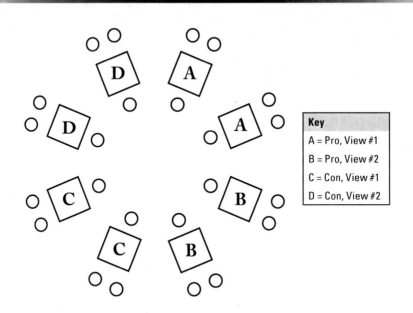

Key

A = Pro, View #1

B = Pro, View #2

C = Con, View #1

D = Con, View #2

The simulation involves having one-third of the students, assigned to each viewpoint, assume the roles of speakers. They can act the part of judges, legislators, lawyers, advocates of a cause, or spokespersons. These students form the inner ring of the circle and face and confront one another in the discussion. Explain that the members of the inner circle of the discussion will be the only ones who talk during the discussion time. The outer ring consists of the remaining two-thirds of the class. These students will act the roles of clerks, advisors, aides, or disseminators of information. It is the clerks' job to use active listening and write suggestions by passing notes to the inner-circle participants. In order to avoid interrupting the flow of conversation, the clerk is encouraged to tap the person's shoulder to notify him or her that there is a note waiting. Without turning around, the student in the inner circle who is actively speaking at the time raises his or her hand to receive the note. After 5 or 10 minutes of active engagement, the inner circle changes places with one of the outer-circle students. This process is rotated until all students have had the chance to sit in the inner circle. Once the activity has been described in detail, you may wish to implement negotiable contracting of assessment so that students are aware of the criteria.

Stix Discussion can take any form, but don't be surprised when a verdict or solution remains elusive. The forum is simply an opportunity for students to speak out, voicing their opinions, hopes, and fears. Whatever choices are selected for a Stix Discussion, it is a strategy that gives students the opportunity to share their thoughts with others as well as learn to make good arguments.

Ideas for Assessment

As each student sits in the inner circle, based on the negotiably contracted criteria, evaluate his or her comments using the following ideas as samples.

- Is the comment relevant?

- Is the comment clear?

- Is the comment persuasive in nature?

- Does the comment make a contribution to the discussion?

These yes and no answers can be used to quickly assess students' participation. It shows where students might need extra help in making their points. One way of helping students is to model a discussion, pointing out strong, relevant comments from ones that are not as strong or relevant. You can also review the discussion with the entire class, pointing out the really strong comments that students made.

After each discussion, ask each group to pass in their clerk notes so that you can review their thoughts. You can also briefly meet for one or two minutes with each group to discuss their participation in the discussion. Have them tell you about the clerk notes at this time.

Applying the Strategy

A Stix Discussion in language arts could take the viewpoints of four different characters in a book. Social studies topics can include events from history and four possible viewpoints about those events. Math discussions could include students designing a new ball park where vendors, observers, team players, and referees would need to have a say in terms of its design. Science topics from the news, like global warming or drilling for natural gas, make great discussions using this strategy.

Interviewing

While good interviewers on television make this skill look easy, it takes practice and strategic planning to master the skill of interviewing. Interviews typically occur between two people. Panels can also participate in an interview of one person. Small groups of people can be interviewed as well. The key to being a good interviewer is being a good listener and allowing the interview to take a journey with unexpected turns if needed.

Knowing how to interview others helps expand students' worlds. They can have the chance to explore the struggles and happiness of other people. They can find out how things get done, who does them, and what occurs as a result. Understanding where others come from makes our lives richer, and others can share the information beyond the two involved in the interview.

How to Do It

To master the art of interviewing, students must first understand the different types of questions (closed- and open-ended questions) and when to use them. As students first begin to practice how to conduct interviews, you should have a lesson or two about these questions. These lessons should cover the difference between closed-ended and open-ended questions by having students identify the differences. Students should think about times when it is appropriate to ask closed-ended questions in an interview because there are appropriate times for both. Furthermore, students need to practice writing these types of questions and asking these types of questions.

The first step in Interviewing is having someone to interview. Assign interview partners to students. Then, show students clips of various interviews conducted by famous individuals and have them analyze the interviews for the styles and types of questions used. It might help if students have a checklist as they are watching the interview. Design the questions correctly with the students. Samples may include, but are not limited to:

- Were the questions mainly open-ended questions?

- When did the interviewer ask follow-up questions?

- When were closed-ended questions asked?

- What theme(s) was the interviewer trying to establish with his or her questions?

- In what ways was the interviewer able to provoke a good discussion rather than just a series of questions and answers?

Students should understand that Interviewing involves doing research. Help them understand ways to get the information so that they are ready for their interviews. This includes finding out the background of a person or a topic. Conduct a mock interview to show students the wrong way to interview a person. Once the activity has been described in detail, implement negotiable contracting of assessment. Have students analyze the mistakes in this interview, like asking questions on a list that the person has already answered, omitting follow-up questions, showing how you did not do your research, and asking too many closed-ended questions. Students should write their own interview questions and have you check them before conducting the interview.

Ideas for Assessment

After the interviews, have students critique their work using a peer or self-assessment form. Students can use the checklist questions mentioned previously, or you can devise a new set of criteria for them to use. Then, students can conference with you in small groups to review their self-assessments.

Finally, have students write short reflections on their interviews to help them improve their interview skills. Use the following question and statement response:

- For what reasons was_____ the strongest point of my interview?
- If I were to relive the experience, here are three things that I would like to change or modify in my technique.

Applying the Strategy

Depending on the topic, interviews can be conducted in any content area. Typical interviews can be conducted around careers, events, or news. For example, if the news is reporting about people who have lost their jobs in your area because of the poor economy, have students find someone to interview who has experienced this and ask them what strategies they used to gain new employment. However, it's also fun to interview characters from a book to make them come alive. Students may also choose to interview scientists, meteorologists, mathematicians, authors, and other people who connect to the other content areas.

Mix Freeze Share

In this discussion strategy, students move around the classroom as music plays. When the music stops, students freeze and wait for a question posed by their teacher-coach. They then share their thoughts about the question with someone standing nearby.

This strategy helps students to mingle with others in the classroom that they might not normally talk to. In the process, it will show them others who have similar ideas or thoughts. It also gives quiet students practice talking to others in a nonthreatening format. An added benefit is that movement is good for learning (Roth 2012). As students converse, it helps them move the knowledge of a topic from abstract to concrete for better comprehension (Jackson 2009).

How to Do It

Begin by selecting a set of questions to ask students about a topic. You can set up these questions as multiple choice, open-ended, yes/no, or explanation. Multiple choice questions work well if you want students to get to know one another. For example:

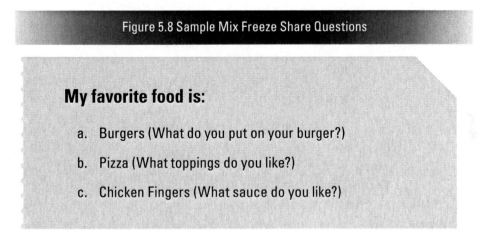

Figure 5.8 Sample Mix Freeze Share Questions

My favorite food is:

a. Burgers (What do you put on your burger?)

b. Pizza (What toppings do you like?)

c. Chicken Fingers (What sauce do you like?)

Open-ended questions offer many responses. For example, *Explain your favorite character and justify your reasoning in detail.* "Do/don't" and "explain" will help students elaborate on a topic. For example, *For what reasons do or don't you agree with the statement . . . Explain why or why not.*

To keep from having to repeat the questions, place the questions on a document camera, an interactive whiteboard, or use PowerPoint® slides and reveal them once students have frozen. Tell students to walk around the room quietly while music plays. Once the music stops, students should freeze in place. When everyone is still, students should look for the person nearest to them and form partners. Announce a question to the class, and then give them some time to think. Students should share their answers with their partners. Set aside one or two minutes for this sharing, depending on the complexity of the question. Once everyone has finished discussing, they should face you. Announce "Mix!" and the students repeat the activity by finding new partners and answering new questions until the activity is over.

Ideas for Assessment

Before embarking on this activity, negotiably contract with students as to what behaviors you will be observing. Quickly glance around the room during the activity to make sure that all students are participating. You can also mingle with students as they are discussing the questions to get a sense of some student discussions and use a performance assessment sheet based on the criteria outlined ahead of time. Another idea is to have students journal or share aloud a few things they learned during the discussion.

Applying the Strategy

Mix Freeze Share strategy can be used with students of all ages and in all content areas. It works especially well in math where students can answer yes or no and explain questions about math problems. For example, a picture of a trapezoid could be shown, and the question might ask students if this shape is a polygon. One student can answer yes or no, and the other student can explain why or why not. It can also be useful in science to review types of trees or make predictions about an experiment on force and motion.

Negotiations and Settlements

What does it take to become a community organizer, a diplomat, a contract lawyer, or an ambassador? It is the art of negotiation. This is not a sports game in which the winner takes all. Instead, it is the ability to realize that there are 150 shades of gray between black and white, and the negotiator cannot come home without a negotiated settlement somewhere in between. The Negotiations and Settlements strategy will place students in that very position, and will assess them on how well they settled a deal.

How to Do It

To begin, discuss with students the area of disagreement where they feel a negotiation is needed. Topics may include but are not limited to where to place the future hospital on a city map, whether Iran should have nuclear capabilities, what grades and departments should be responsible for a schoolwide Thanksgiving feast, or how much money should be allotted to NASA's space program when the federal school budget has been slashed.

Within each cooperative group of four students, two students sitting side by side represent one point of view and the two students sitting opposite them represent the opposing viewpoint. Inform students that they are delegates/ambassadors and it is their job to negotiate a treaty. They don't want to fail at this task because they could risk losing their diplomatic positions. It will be their job to research the topic from as many viewpoints as possible so that they can be adequately prepared for their position. Many sources should be utilized from books, media clips, apps, articles, and blogs.

Each pair should iron out its point of view before generating a list of points and demands that will give them a treaty they desire. Then, the two pairs discuss and try to work out a compromise and negotiate a final treaty that satisfies both positions. Allow students to negotiate a deal for the rest of the period. As students work out their treaties, the teacher-coach circulates among the groups giving help and assistance. Notify students when there are 10 minutes left in the period. Let them know that when the five-minute mark is called out, they should try to be finished and be ready to write down their compromise in the proper quadrant. Call out the five-minute mark and allow students to fill out the quadrant on the chart. For homework, ask students to reflect on the experience.

At the next class period, call upon one speaker from each cooperative group at a time. All other groups must listen and must chart the negotiation in preparation for a vote. This will ensure that the class implements "active listening." Continue this process until all groups have presented. Allow the class to compare the notes from each group. Ask the class to individually rank the negotiations. This permits students to review the information as well as evaluate the treaties. It is important to not have one group be a winner in this exercise, as your goal as a teacher-coach is to instill self-confidence in all pupils that their efforts were justly made. Share the rankings with each group, based on the negotiated criteria that were made. It is imperative to note that if all groups made a treaty, then they were all winners. However, the winner is the group that did the most research and applied their skills to come up with an agreement.

Ask students to reflect on the negotiating process. You may also want students to compare and contrast the actual historical outcome to their personal experiences for journal-writing purposes. For homework, students use newspapers, magazines, blogs, and periodicals to find treaties that are being negotiated today in some parts of the world. You may choose to post newspaper clippings next to the map of the world. A string may be used to connect the clipping to the actual location of the region that is the subject of the negotiations.

Ideas for Assessment

Before students begin working, start negotiable contracting on how they would assess the treaties if they were the teacher. As the teacher-coach, you will use these student-generated criteria as a form of performance assessment. Some examples are as follows:

- Works collaboratively
- Uses persuasive language
- Uses language that is respectful, not argumentative
- Uses the facts needed to make the compromise

Topic:	Works Collaboratively	Uses Persuasive Language	Is Respectful of Others	Makes Effort to Compromise
Student's Name:				
1.				
2.				
3.				

Group #1: Negotiated Points:		
•		
•		
•		
Group #2: Negotiated Points:		
•		
•		
•		

Provide a chart on which students write down critical information as a form of peer assessment. Inform them that they will need to write down the negotiated agreement in the proper quadrant at the end of the negotiation.

Discuss how to take notes, or briefly write down in two or three words the description of a sentence. It is recommended that you first model this on the board. After modeling, create a "negotiable contract," so that students know how they are being graded on the chart paper. For example, the teacher asks students what criteria they would use to assess the charts if they were the teacher. Some suggestions may be:

- Writing is easy to understand
- Succinct and to the point
- Represents the negotiation
- Sequential and organized
- Represents a compromised solution

Names of Students:	Writing Is Easy to Understand	Is Succinct and to the Point	Represents the Negotiation	Is Sequential and Organized	Represents a Compromised Solution
Comments for Students:					

Applying the Strategy

The Negotiations and Settlements strategy works well in all content areas. However, it especially lends itself to be used in social studies. If students were actually negotiating a treaty from a historical time period, then the teacher could compare their treaty with the original one. Therefore, be sure to change the name of the treaty before you begin. You don't want students looking up the answer beforehand.

The topics may include royalties on music on the Internet, author's rights in digital media, and the rights of cloning in science. A language arts teacher may set up a negotiation topic (conflict) found in a book and let students decide on how it will be resolved. The topics for this strategy are endless!

Tic-Tac-Toe

A Tic-Tac-Toe uses a tic-tac-toe grid with nine questions or topics written on it. Each student finds another student and selects a square from the grid with a question for that student to answer. Once a correct answer is given, the student writes an *X* on the square and moves on to find another student.

This discussion strategy gets students talking to one another. As the students seek out others to answer various questions on their tic-tac-toe boards, the content is reinforced and reviewed. They also have the practice of answering the questions given on other boards. A teacher-coach can design a few different tic-tac-toe boards for differentiation. You may decide to review questions ahead of time with the students for clarification before they begin the actual strategy. Tic-Tac-Toe can be used in small groups, with teams, with partners, or individually.

How to Do It

To begin, decide on nine discussion questions and write each one in a different section of a tic-tac-toe board. These questions can be from any content area and can be fact-based or open-ended. Open-ended questions make for better discussions among students. For example, a fact-based question in science could be to name a predator of a snake. An open-ended question could be to tell one consequence that might occur if the predator of a snake were to suddenly become extinct.

Give every student (group or partner) a tic-tac-toe board. Tell each student to select a question from the tic-tac-toe board to present to another student to answer, or tell the student that they can select a question not already answered from the board. This works well for struggling students since they can select the questions they feel confident answering. Students should place an *X* on the selected question that is answered, but we recommend that you make the board large enough for students to write key points from their peer's answer on the board. Then, that student should move on to ask a different student a new question. Each student plays until all the squares have been answered. You may wish to implement negotiable contracting of assessment once the activity has been described in detail to students.

Ideas for Assessment

If using this as a review activity, give a quick, short quiz to review the content that students just discussed with others during this activity. This quiz can help you know what needs to be reviewed again before students are tested on the content. The tic-tac-toe board on *Charlotte's Web* by E.B. White could look like the chart in Figure 5.9. Then, these same questions could be given in a short quiz to make sure students understand the content of the story. If students do poorly on the quiz, take the time to reteach or conduct a whole-group discussion using the tic-tac-toe board.

Figure 5.9 Sample Charlotte's Web Tic-Tac-Toe Board

Q: If you were Charlotte, what would you write in Wilbur's web at the fair? Explain. **A:**	**Q:** In what ways is Templeton a good guy or a bad guy in this story? Explain. **A:**	**Q:** Why does Charlotte like Wilbur? **A:**
Q: Describe in detail what qualities make Charlotte a good friend. **A:**	**Q:** Explain specifically two things that good friends do for one another. **A:**	**Q:** Why does Fern care so much about Wilbur? **A:**
Q: What else could Charlotte have written in the web to help Wilbur? **A:**	**Q:** What lesson can we learn from this story? **A:**	**Q:** How does another character (besides Charlotte or Templeton) help Wilbur? **A:**

Applying the Strategy

This strategy works really well for review games. A tic-tac-toe board can have math problems, science or social studies review questions, or vocabulary questions written on it. You can even have students discuss a poem that they read as a class using this strategy.

Four Corners Discussion

The Four Corners Discussion was adapted from the Academic Controversy strategy (Herreid 1996) and is built around four answer choices, each one represented in a different corner of the room. Once students make a decision to select one of the answers, they move to the corner of the room that represents that answer. In their corners, students hold a discussion about why they selected the particular answer. Finally, students share aloud from the corners and have the chance to change their minds about their final answers.

Four Corners Discussion gives teacher-coaches immediate feedback as they see students moving to one of the four corners. Whether there are right or wrong answers, it gives teacher-coaches a quick snapshot of how students think about a topic. It also can provide students with an unexpected sense of camaraderie among classmates as they participate with others who think similarly.

How to Do It

To begin, create some content area questions about a topic, making sure that students can have four different responses, not just *yes* or *no* but shades of gray as well. It is usually best to think of this in terms of multiple-choice answers. For example, when referring to the story of *Goldilocks and the Three Bears*, students could be asked, *Is it okay for someone like Goldilocks to enter the home of strangers without permission, eat their food, and use their furniture?* This example shows an open-ended question with four possible answers. Students will have to discuss why they selected their answers and what would happen next in the story.

Four corners would include:

a. It is okay to enter the home of strangers, eat all of their food, and use their furniture.

b. It is okay to enter the home of strangers, but you should be careful not to eat all of their food or damage their furniture.

c. It is okay to enter the home of strangers, but you shouldn't touch anything while you're there.

d. It is never okay to enter the home of strangers without permission.

With these statements, students must select a response and discuss it in their corners. To begin:

1. Gather students in the center of the room.

2. Model this activity so that all students will be clear before the activity begins.

3. Read the question or statement, and then post each answer in each corner.

4. Give students a minute to think about their possible answer, and then tell students to move to the corner that best represents his or her opinion.

5. Give students in each corner time to discuss their opinions and to explain why they selected this one over the others.

6. Have each corner share aloud a few of their best opinions.

7. Once every corner has shared, ask students if any of them have changed their minds and would like to move to a new corner. Allow them to move, and then have them explain why they changed their minds.

8. This activity can be repeated with new questions as needed.

Once the activity has been described in detail to students, you may wish to implement negotiable contracting of assessment. The teacher-coach can walk around charting how well students are engaging in the activity based on the criteria of the discussion. Samples may include listening skills, speaking clearly, and providing evidence to support his or her opinion.

Ideas for Assessment

This strategy gives teacher-coaches a quick visual of how their students think about a topic. By asking questions that clarify student thinking, a teacher-coach can find out why a student made a particular decision. To keep track, a teacher-coach can use a classroom map with corners noted on it. Write student names, initials, or student numbers in each corner to show where he or she ended up. In the following science example, a teacher-coach would need to make sure that all students are accounted for in the map. It shows the four corners and the students who selected each corner. Keep notes in each section as students explain the reasons for their decisions.

Figure 5.10 Sample Four Corners Observation Form

Question: Describe in detail what you think will happen in the experiment.	

Corner 1: The mixture will form clumps.
    Susana
    Hannah
    Mike
	Corner 2: The mixture will explode.
	    Ashley

Corner 3: The mixture will dissolve.
    Jake
    Alejandro
    Pricilla
	Corner 4: Nothing will happen.
	    Sean
	    Jackie

Criteria for success during this discussion can be decided upon using the process of negotiable contracting (described in Chapter 1). Possible criteria can include listening skills, speaking skills, and providing evidence of your opinion.

Applying the Strategy

In science class, ask students what they think will happen before the experiment is performed. Give students four choices to choose from, and have them explain their choices in the four corners. Then, perform the experiment and see who was correct. In language arts, pose four possible reasons why a protagonist acted in a specific manner. In math, students can discuss the layout and design of an urban center and discuss what type of building should be highlighted.

Conclusion

Students need to develop strong discussion skills in order to be better communicators. Developing the ability to persuade others, explain viewpoints, and listen to diverse points of view will help students as they grow up and enter the workforce as adults. The strategies in this chapter will help toward that goal.

Let's Think and Discuss

1. Considering your class, which of these strategies will work best with their personalities and abilities?

2. Explain in detail some possible topics you could use with these discussion strategies.

3. Keeping your students in mind, what will be your greatest obstacle to having productive discussions using these strategies? How can you overcome this obstacle?

Decision-Making Strategies

Each and every day we make decisions, some of which have big impacts on our lives. This reality stresses the importance of developing strong decision-making skills. According to decision theorists, decision making is defined as the practice of making choices among contending courses of action. Decision-making skills take problem solving one step further (Raiffa 1968; Von Winterfeldt and Edwards 1986). As in problem solving, decision making involves evaluating possible courses of action. However, decision making must weigh conflicting objectives before deciding on a possible solution. And decision making evaluates each course of action simultaneously. Decision making focuses on a clear goal or outcome.

The College and Career Readiness Anchor Standards focus on helping students be critical thinkers as they analyze and synthesize (CCSS 2010). Many of these opportunities for critical thinking arise as students are faced with decisions and learn how to navigate to make the best decisions. Today, there are so many more choices than there were for our parents and grandparents. Students need to learn how to navigate through choices so that they are prepared for adulthood. Learning decision-making skills can also help students overcome peer pressure. Learning to evaluate possible outcomes as a result of their actions might help steer them away from making harmful, life-altering decisions.

Such decision-making skills do not have to be limited to older students and adolescents. Young students can learn them, too. Begin by giving students a limited number of choices from which to select. These choices may first be based on preferences (e.g., *Do you like this or that better?*) and then can become more complex. For example, teachers can provide students with frames of reference by asking them how other students who are affected by the choice might feel. Guide students to understand how their choices have consequences. As students grow older, this can be implemented even more. This chapter reviews six different strategies that can be effective venues for teaching decision-making skills. They include:

Decisions, Decisions

Decisions, Decisions, a strategy developed by Andi Stix and Frank Hrbek, is based on the idea of multiple endings and outcomes that depend on the reader's decisions. Students will be creating their own "stories" from a series of decisions that result in multiple endings. Then, students reflect on their decisions.

At the very heart of this strategy are decision-making skills. Students' decisions directly affect the outcomes, and students have the opportunity to reflect on what occurs as a result.

How to Do It

Introduce students to this strategy by reading a scenario to them and have them make a decision between two choices. Create selected endings to help students in this process. This is particularly important if the outcomes must be definitive. Based on that decision, another scenario will occur. Students will make another decision between two options (see Figure 6.1). This process can continue or end at any point and allow students to reach the conclusion or story ending.

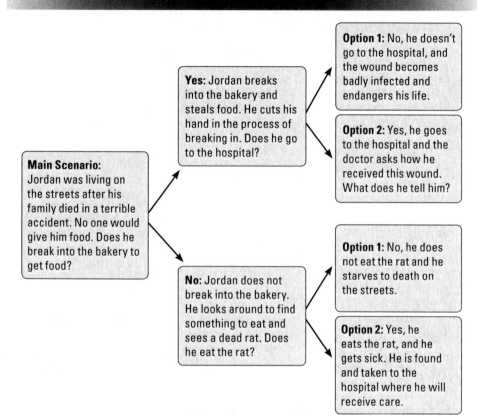

Figure 6.1 Decisions, Decisions Diagram

Main Scenario: Jordan was living on the streets after his family died in a terrible accident. No one would give him food. Does he break into the bakery to get food?

Yes: Jordan breaks into the bakery and steals food. He cuts his hand in the process of breaking in. Does he go to the hospital?

Option 1: No, he doesn't go to the hospital, and the wound becomes badly infected and endangers his life.

Option 2: Yes, he goes to the hospital and the doctor asks how he received this wound. What does he tell him?

No: Jordan does not break into the bakery. He looks around to find something to eat and sees a dead rat. Does he eat the rat?

Option 1: No, he does not eat the rat and he starves to death on the streets.

Option 2: Yes, he eats the rat, and he gets sick. He is found and taken to the hospital where he will receive care.

If desired, take this strategy a step further by having students construct their own Decisions, Decisions stories. It is helpful if students use graphic organizers to help them organize their stories into parts where the reader can make choices. The basic outline of writing this type of story is as follows; First, students must begin a story introduction that grabs the reader's attention. Next, the reader will make a decision. The story continues in two threads. The reader will make another decision. Then, the story will end with at least four possible threads. Assign a length for students to write and explain how their work will be assessed. Students will need time to write their stories. If they don't finish it in class, assign it for homework. Have students peer-edit and make revisions to their stories as needed. Have students test their stories before drafting the final product. Oversee this process. Students should write final copies of their stories. When students finish their stories, have them form small groups to read and share their stories. Once the activity has been explained to students and before embarking on the task, implement negotiable contracting of assessment.

Ideas for Assessment

Students should reflect on their outcomes in classroom discussions and through individual writing. First, have a class or small-group discussion about the results of the activity. Use the following questions to guide the discussion:

- In what ways were the outcomes in the story similar to or different from the expected outcomes?

- If you had to redo the exercise, in what ways would you change or modify it?

- For what reasons might these modifications have made this story better?

Then, have students write short journal reflections on their stories and the experience of this activity. This reflection should include what they would do differently next time in their own writing pieces. Finally, use a rubric similar to the one in Figure 6.2 using the negotiated criteria and point values for each criterion.

Figure 6.2 Sample Decisions, Decisions Rubric

Criteria	Points
Graphic organizer was completed	
Story introduction grabs the reader's attention	
The reader must make *at least* two decisions during the story	
The story ends with four possible threads	
Total:	

Vote on It

Vote on It is an activity in which students participate in a task in which they determine the best choice for a given situation. Students are given choices on cards, such as a group of resumes, and must evaluate them and vote for the best one.

This activity challenges students' evaluation skills through a higher-order thinking activity. Students learn to grapple with hard decisions and, in the process, confront their own biases. What were their reasons for making their decision? What compelled them to make that decision? Critical thinking goes into high gear as students analyze this information. Students also rank the selections from the best to the worst selections and must defend their choices. Most importantly, students make decisions and have to back them up with reasons based on the information given on the choice cards.

How to Do It

Begin by creating a scenario that asks students to choose the best option from six choices. The vote can be for people, ideas, or another topic. Make a profile card (see Figures 6.3 and 6.4) for each of the six selections. Make sure to withhold key information that would give away the secret identity on the profile cards. For example, the titles or people's names are often omitted from the profile cards. Instead of voting for a particular person, students are forced to look at the qualifications of the "mystery" person.

Figure 6.3 Sample Profile Card 1

Presidential Candidate Résumés

Résumé #1

Education: formal education until age 16; professional orator; gave speeches that captured people's attention and inspired them; studied and appreciated the arts; had aspirations to be an artist; published author

Experience: served his country bravely in a major war; had many harrowing escapes from death during the war; received a total of five medals in the war; active political party member; political fundraiser; sought-after public speaker

Background: homeless early in life; nonsmoker and nondrinker; single; no children

Age: 56 years old

Résumé #2

Education: no formal education as a child; thought to be dyslexic; graduated from Princeton University; attended law school for a brief period of time; earned Ph.D. from Johns Hopkins University

Experience: college professor; president of Princeton University; state governor; authored a best-sellng book; successful at planning legislation for the working man; sought-after public speaker

Background: father was a Presbyterian minister; married two times; one child

Age: 57 years old

Tell students that you will show them six profile cards and they must select the best one from the list. Students must work with the information provided to make their choices. The goal is that students discuss their viewpoints and biases to find the best-fit qualities.

A vote is taken after students have time to review the profile cards. Students can cast a written vote, or they can vote by a show of hands. Students can only vote once for their favorite. Tally the votes for the favorite and least favorite and announce them to the class. You may wish to implement negotiable contracting of assessments so that students are familiar with the expectations of the assignment.

Ideas for Assessment

Have students discuss why they made their selections. This reflection opens the doors to talk about biases. You can have students write about or discuss the following:

- Describe specifically what was appealing about each profile card.

- Explain in detail what résumé cards might be missing that warrants a person's interview.

At the very end of the activity, reveal the answers that correspond to each profile card. Below is a sample profile card with all the information disclosed.

Figure 6.4 Sample Profile Card 2

Profile Cards

Résumé #2

- learned under his father's guidance

- graduated from Princeton University and earned a Ph.D. from Johns Hopkins University

- served as a college professor at both Bryn Mawr and Princeton University

- became president of Princeton University

- elected governor of New Jersey

- authored a best-selling book

- passed legislation for the working man

- elected as the twenty-eighth president of the United States

- excellent public speaker; traveled promoting his Fourteen Points

Woodrow Wilson

Applying the Strategy

Vote on It can be used in any of the content areas. In social studies, this strategy can be used to compare leaders within a certain era. In language arts, Vote on It can be used to analyze characters in a play. In science, students could vote on infectious diseases to eradicate first. In math, students vote on the best design.

Identity Crisis

In the Identity Crisis strategy, a mystery identity is placed on students' backs, so each student cannot see his or her own identity. By asking questions of their fellow students, each student tries to determine the mystery "person or thing" from among the many important people, figures, or topics unique to what the class is studying. This strategy reinforces what students have already been learning about people, figures, or topics. It can be used as an activity at the end of a unit of study or as the assessment of that study.

Identity Crisis uses deductive reasoning. Reasoning is the process of drawing conclusions or inferences from information. It requires going beyond information that is given. Students have to use the information from their reasoning to make decisions about the types of questions they ask next to determine their secret identity. The goal is to ask as few questions as possible to reach their identity. This emphasizes the art of making good decisions about the questions that should be asked.

How to Do It

1. Begin by giving students a study guide or review that they can use to prepare for the Identity Crisis activity.

2. Then, prepare the identity cards. These cards can be large index note cards, 8.5" × 11" paper, or 8" × 10" pieces of poster board. If these identity cards will be used more than once, laminate them to make them more durable.

3. Punch two holes in the top of the cards and string with yarn to make a necklace that is long enough to slide over the heads of the students. Students will wear it like a backward necklace.

4. Then, the cards can be placed directly on the backs of students.

These identity cards should have the name of the identity as well as a brief description of the person or thing. If you have more students in the class than identities, make as many sets of the identity cards to have enough for all your students and create cooperative groups. If applicable, a picture or an image of the identity can be placed on the cards as well. The following example shows identity cards created on the American Civil War generals and officers (see Figure 6.5).

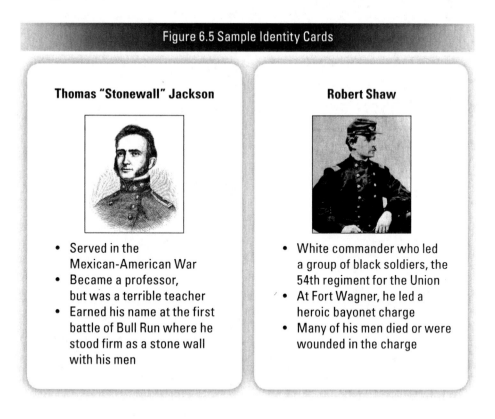

Figure 6.5 Sample Identity Cards

Thomas "Stonewall" Jackson

- Served in the Mexican-American War
- Became a professor, but was a terrible teacher
- Earned his name at the first battle of Bull Run where he stood firm as a stone wall with his men

Robert Shaw

- White commander who led a group of black soldiers, the 54th regiment for the Union
- At Fort Wagner, he led a heroic bayonet charge
- Many of his men died or were wounded in the charge

On the activity day, give students time to prepare questions they will ask during the activity. Students should seek to ask questions that can eliminate several possibilities at the same time. Explain that these questions must be answered by other students with either "yes" or "no." For example, *Am I in the Union Army?* Remind students that even though they have prepared good questions, they will still have to make smart decisions when asking questions based on the answers they receive.

Once they have prepared good questions, give each student an identity card and place them on students' backs so that each student cannot see his or her own identity. Explain that students will act as both a questioner and someone who answers questions in this activity. As a questioner, they will only be allowed to ask each student two questions before having to move on to a new person. If they are the person who answers the questions, then they should look at the Identity Crisis card on the back of the questioner to see the answer and the clues so that they can answer the questions correctly.

Give students a time limit of 10 minutes, and allow them to ask their questions. If they correctly guess their identities, they can still answer questions. Once the activity has been described in detail to students, you may implement negotiable contracting of assessments.

Ideas for Assessment

Once everyone correctly identifies his or her identity, have students analyze their list of questions again. What would they change, and what would they keep the same?

Have students list their two top questions (even a revised question) and write why these questions are the best for determining the identities that were assigned to them. This can be turned in so that the teacher can see student thought processes. Make short notes to keep track of student progress, and provide students with feedback in the form of comments either verbally or written. The goal is for students to write questions that will help them with their logical ability to keep negating possibilities so that they can narrow down their choice of an answer. Use this assessment to measure student progress the next time the strategy is used.

Applying the Strategy

Identity Crisis can be used in all content areas. In language arts, use it to study vocabulary words, book characters, or parts of speech. Geography topics include places and landforms, and social studies topics can include people as well as events in history. This strategy can be used in math, where students must come up with the identification of shapes or their geometric understanding. Science can include the identification of landforms, crystals, and species.

Mystery Boxes

Mystery Boxes is an activity in which each student decorates a box to show a particular topic without explicitly writing the topic heading or title. The box should be decorated on the outside with clues or clever hints about the topic.

Mystery Boxes are ideal for getting students to think deductively to make good decisions. Deductive thinking is characterized by elimination. It is the "if this, then that" type of thinking. In the real world, a person might be given some clues and then must use those clues to come to a logical conclusion or decision. This strategy will give students the opportunity to develop those skills.

How to Do It

Begin by explaining that students will create a mystery box for a secret topic assigned to each of them. You can do this by having each student draw a slip of paper with a topic on it from a bag. Have students individually brainstorm a list of ways that the topic can be represented on their boxes without showing their list to others. For example, students can draw pictures or icons, use magazine images or clip art, or write slogans or words.

Students might need some time to research their topics, so allow them time either at home or school to do so. Set a due date for the Mystery Boxes. On the day of the activity, place students in groups of four. Assign each student a different number. If there are 20 students in class, each student should have a number from 1–20. If a card happens to fall on the floor and you don't notice it until later, it would take too long to figure out to which cooperative group it belongs

Part of this assignment includes writing about the topic in at least four paragraphs without mentioning the topic by name. This will be part of the mystery that others will solve, too. You can edit the papers or have students edit each other's papers. Since students will have to place the paragraphs in order, have them think of words that will help the reader. Words like *next, moreover, in conclusion,* or *finally* aid the reader. Once papers are in final form, distribute small index cards. Students should write their assigned number on the back of all four index cards. This way, the cards can be correctly identified with the appropriate Mystery Boxes.

All paragraphs should be typed out using the same font style, font size, and margins. Students can cut out each paragraph and glue it on each card. The back side of each card should be lettered *A, B, C,* or *D* to serve as an answer key, next to the student number so that it will read *1A, 1B,* etc. These should be due on the same day as the Mystery Boxes.

Have each group place index cards faceup in a pile and shuffle the pile. Each student should have his or her box on the table. Rotate all groups to new tables, so they will not interact with their own Mystery Boxes. Students enjoy getting out of their chairs and moving to a new location. It also increases blood flow to the brain, which energizes students. At the new tables, students should take turns drawing a card from the pile and trying to match it to the correct box. Once they believe they have a match, they should slide it into the box. When all the cards have been placed inside the boxes, allow students to check inside the box to see if the number on all four note cards matches the number inside the box. If not, have the group work together to place the note cards into the correct mystery box.

Finally, students should try to guess which topic each box is representing. Once students have finished, rotate the groups to another table where they will interact with a new set of Mystery Boxes. Repeat this activity until students have visited all the Mystery Boxes, including their own. Once the activity has been explained in detail and before they embark on the task, begin negotiable contracting of assessment.

Ideas for Assessment

Once the activity is complete, assign students to one of the tables they visited. Have them select different Mystery Boxes to assess. Explain that each of them must provide detailed information about the mystery box. Use negotiable contracting of assessment to allow students input in deciding the criteria for success. This information will help the creator of the box to know what they need to improve for next time. It is important for students to provide an idea or two in the comments section for improving the box. Use the following criteria as a guide for student feedback.

Figure 6.6 Sample Mystery Box Assessment			
The outside of the mystery box provides clues to the identity	Circle: Yes / No		
Four index cards with written clues are included	Circle: Yes / No		
Circle the best answer:	The topic was too easy to guess	The topic was somewhat challenging	The topic was challenging, but the clues helped	The topic was too difficult to guess
Provide at least two comments about the mystery box.	Comment 1:		Comment 2:

Applying the Strategy

This strategy will work with all content areas. A student assigned a type of figurative language could decorate the box with examples or pictures that demonstrate that specific figurative language. For example, a student might decorate a box about idioms with images of cats and dogs raining from the sky as well as sayings like, *She was so hungry she could eat a horse*. Vocabulary words in any content area can be used for Mystery Boxes as well as characters from books. A math concept like shapes in real life can be depicted on Mystery Boxes. Boxes can even represent real people like scientists or historical figures as well as ecosystems, landforms, and geographical places.

The Sorting Bag

The Sorting Bag activity offers students the opportunity to discuss the classification of diverse items that have been placed in bags. Each small group of students receives a bag with various items related to the content of study. Students work together to sort these items into groups, thus classifying the items and giving reasons for their decisions. The ultimate goal is that students discuss and give reasons for their answers while learning new vocabulary and concepts related to their classification.

This strategy supports visual spatial learners because of the tactile items included in the bags. Students are engaged and motivated because the activity is hands-on in nature (Bass, Yumol, and Hazer 2012). They have the opportunity to practice using new vocabulary and concepts as they discuss and can relate these new words to the content readily with repeated practice. Finally, the activity is open-ended, so there will be ample opportunity for students to practice creative thinking as they construct the classifications and critical reasoning and explain their reasons for the classification.

How to Do It

Decide upon items that relate to the content your class is studying. Place the items in paper bags. These items can be pictures, word cards, and objects. Each bag can be a little different from another.

Begin by modeling this activity for students so that they understand the expectations. Then, place students with partners or in small groups of three students per group. Give each group a bag with items and tell them to work in their groups to classify (group) the items in their bags. As they work, they should discuss their decisions with their group members. Students should have 5 to 10 minutes to work with their groups. Give students a three-minute warning before the time runs out.

When the time is up, each group will explain their classification system, giving reasons for each category. Students should clarify how the grouped items relate to one another. As students explain their classification system, be on the lookout for opportunities to introduce new vocabulary and concepts. Write these key words on the board so that students can reference them. Then, allow students to reclassify their items according to what they have learned about new vocabulary and concepts. You may wish to implement negotiable contracting of assessments once the activity has been described to students and before implementation.

Ideas for Assessment

As a final activity, have the class summarize what they have learned by writing key points on large paper and displaying them for the class. To encourage differentiation, this can be done pictorially or as graphic organizers, beside the standard way of writing lists. Again, encourage them to include the new concepts and vocabulary words in their summary. The information that students provide will inform the teacher if concepts need to be taught again, should be reinforced, or if students are ready to move on to a new topic.

Applying the Strategy

Students can classify shapes, numbers, stickers, or other items in math class. In science, students can sort rocks of various sizes and textures. Use large paper bags and fill them with photocopies of book covers, miniatures, and books that can be sorted according to the characters or settings. Historical items like old money and artifacts can be placed in bags for students to sort and classify. A favorite of ours is to classify a mystery person's garbage so that the students can identify the person. This is a great way of learning about social studies and objects that once existed. Students can also find something from their book bag and place it on the counter to be sorted.

Matching Cards

Matching Cards is a strategy that has students looking for the matching concept to the cards they have been given. The strategy can be designed to have one correct answer, or it can be open-ended, with several correct answers.

This strategy supports visual learners because the words are written on the cards (pictures can be used for very young learners). It also supports English language learners as they practice the language while they work with others to see if their cards are true matches. Even very young students get practice making decisions as they participate in this activity.

How to Do It

To begin, prepare sets of Matching Cards so each student can have one card related to concepts being studied. Depending on the content, some of these cards can be open-ended, having many possible answers. Let students know if there is more than one possible answer. See Figure 6.7 for sample matching cards.

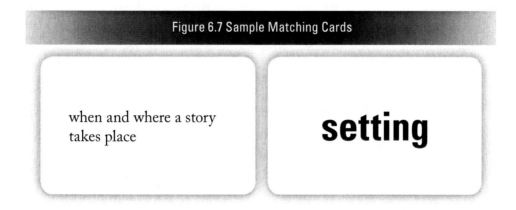

Figure 6.7 Sample Matching Cards

when and where a story takes place

setting

Give each student a card. As a variation, place students in pairs or small groups instead of having them work individually. Then, students in each group will support one another as they look for a match to their card. Instruct students to walk around the class and match their card to another student's card. Once they think they have found a match, they should have a discussion to make sure they have the right match.

This strategy can be modified by giving multiple cards to each pair of students and having them group the cards into categories. Students may also order the cards sequentially or in a time line, design a puzzle, select their favorite or least favorite, link the cards according to an attribute, select a card according to a character's profile, scramble and unscramble them, or even design a slogan out of them.

Ideas for Assessment

Decide if you want students to explain their answers to only you or if they will share them with others. Typically, the entire class can benefit from all the concepts, so have students share aloud their reasons for their matches. Older students can share their answers in small groups. Be sure to circle around the room to hear their reasoning.

Applying the Strategy

This strategy can be used with math facts and equations, causes and effects, characters and descriptions, and vocabulary in any content area. The possibilities with this strategy are endless.

Conclusion

It is essential for students to develop strong decision-making skills. The ability to make good sound decisions will aid students their entire lives. The strategies in this chapter are designed to give students practice with making decisions through deductive reasoning. The Decisions, Decisions strategy not only helps students see consequences of their choices, but it also gives them the opportunity to design and write their own adventure. Through deductive reasoning, students find out how their decisions affect the outcomes. Vote on It shows students their biases as well as things to look for in a good "candidate." In this sense, deductive reasoning is used as students decide on the best candidates based on their résumés. Identity Crisis gives students the chance to write good questions that can eliminate more than one answer to reach the correct one. The process of elimination in this way is a classic example of deductive reasoning. Mystery Boxes allow students to design clues that point to a mystery identity represented in a box and written paragraphs. This forces others to use deductive reasoning as they seek to guess the mysterious identity. The Sorting Bag introduces students to the very basics of classification, and the Matching Cards strategy benefits students by having them share reasons for their decisions. These are both great introduction activities to getting younger students to think deductively.

Let's Think and Discuss

1. Describe in detail which decision-making strategy would benefit your students most, and why.

2. What are some possible topics for using a strategy from this chapter in your class?

3. In what ways can you plan to use Sorting Bag with your students?

Chapter

Strategies for Creative and Dramatic Arts

Strategies that promote creative and dramatic arts benefit students academically, communally, and personally. Academically, creative and dramatic arts are avenues for higher-level thinking in which students take information, interpret it, and then do something with it creatively to demonstrate their understanding (Silverstein and Layne 2010). Silverstein and Layne (2010) make the case that "Arts integration provides multiple ways for students to make sense of what they learn (construct understanding) and makes their learning visible (demonstrate understanding). It goes beyond the initial step of helping students learn and recall information to challenging students to take the information and facts they have learned and do something with them to build deeper understanding." Donovan and Pascale (2012) say that creative and dramatic arts demand that students "translate their understanding of content into new forms… In order to move between languages and symbol systems to create new representations, students must draw upon higher-order critical thinking skills such as analysis and evaluation, leading to artistic creation. In poetry, students use words in new ways that are fresh and derive new meaning; in drama they explore ideas through character, dramatic context, and multiple perspectives. Visual art harnesses the power of metaphor, and movement boils concepts down into their essence in ways that defy literal interpretation. Students translate information into new forms, blending ideas with their own unique perspectives, background experiences, voice, and talent" (Donovan and Pascale 2012, 18).

Communally, these strategies help students to understand that there are multiple perspectives, and in turn, students can become more empathetic and understanding. "Learning to look through multiple perspectives, young people may be helped to build bridges among themselves; attending to a range of human stories, they may be provoked to heal and transform" (Green 1992, 16).

The creative and dramatic arts strategies included in this chapter are:

- Playlets and Puppetry (page 137)
- Total Physical Response (page 140)
- Rapping, Rhyming, and Singing (page 141)
- Gallery Walk, Museum Exhibit, or Fair (page 144)
- Newscasts, Newspapers, and Slide Show Alive (page 147)
- Fan Fold Designs (page 150)
- Molding Dough Sculptures (page 156)

Strategies that promote the creative and dramatic arts support many learning styles. These experiences help make for more well-rounded students who feel confident taking on these challenges when they arise. The ability to do these things well will set students apart from others, especially in the workplace. To excel in these areas, students need practice doing them. For example, Fan Fold Designs and Molding Dough Sculptures meet the needs of visual spatial learners and allows them to express their understanding visually and artistically. Gallery Walk, Rapping, Rhyming, and Singing, Playlets and Puppetry, and Newscasts and Newspapers give students practice in public speaking and performing as well as practice writing for audiences. Total Physical Response and many of these previously mentioned strategies provide kinesthetic learners the necessary movement for learning and understanding. All these strategies give students practice in both creative and dramatic arts and are included in this chapter.

For students who seem reluctant to try these, there are a few things teacher-coaches can do. First, teacher-coaches need to reassure students that there is not one correct way to show artistically what they know or have learned. There are many different answers, and depending on students' personalities and strengths, they will show these differently. Teacher-coaches can also participate in the activity or show an example they created before students begin. This shows that the teacher-coach is willing to be vulnerable, too, and helps those who are unsure of the expectations to feel safe as they create. Finally, teacher-coaches can partner up students to create together. This gives reluctant students the confidence they need when they begin working individually on these projects.

Playlets and Puppetry

Playlets and Puppetry are strategies that encourage full participation of all students. In both of these strategies, students fashion the dialogues, costumes, and settings as they write their own scripts to teach about a certain topic or event. An event can be reenacted in a play or a puppet show, or these strategies can be used to creatively talk or teach about a topic.

How to Do It

Decide if students will be performing plays or puppet shows. If students perform puppet shows, they will need to create puppets as characters. These puppets can be as simple as finger puppets, lunch bags, or sock puppets. If students perform plays, they will need to consider costumes and props to enhance the plays. See Figure 7.1 for examples of puppets.

Figure 7.1 Sample Puppets

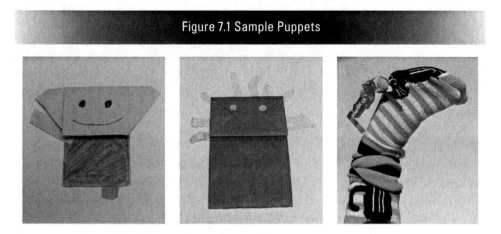

Then, decide if students will work individually or in groups of two to four students. If working in groups, all students in the groups must participate. Set a time limit for the performances. For example, the performances should be under four minutes in length.

First, students should brainstorm about the topics. What are all the possible ways they could cover their content? Explain to students that they will take this idea of talking about a subject to create scripts for the performances. All students should share in the writing of the scripts. Show students a sample of a script so that they will understand how to write it.

Sample Script

Dr. Flats: Now, tell me what Willie and Fred did to make themselves flat.

Fred's Mom: The boys slept with a heavy mattress on top of them.

Dr. Flats: That reminds me of a book I just read to my son about a boy. He flattened himself using a bulletin board.

Fred's Mom: It sounds like these boys got their flat scheme from the book *Flat Stanley*. Please tell me you have a cure for this awful flatness!

Dr. Flats: I am sorry to say that there is no cure for flatness.

(Adapted from Conklin 2004)

Make sure that students understand how their performances will be assessed. Once the activity has been described in detail to students, you may implement negotiable contracting of assessments. Set a due date, and give students time to work on their written scripts. Students can complete work in class or for homework. Students will also need to practice for the performances.

On the day of the activity, call each group forward and have them perform for the class. Close the activity by having students discuss their performances, talking about what they liked most, what they liked least, and what they learned from the experience.

Ideas for Assessment

A rubric for performing a play could look like the following example. This example examines the content, props, and audience's attention. A rubric could also analyze the costumes, facial expressions, voice, and facts.

Figure 7.2 Sample Playlets and Puppetry Rubric

	Novice	Apprentice	Proficient	Distinguished
Content	The play is not related to the content at all.	The play is somewhat related to the content but does not fully explain it.	The play is clearly related to the content and topic and fully explains it.	The play is clearly related to the content and topic. Great detail is included.
Props	Students do not use any props.	Students use few props to enhance the play.	Students use several props to enhance their play.	Students use wonderfully detailed props that extend the story.
Interest	Students did not hold the audience's attention at all.	Students held the audience's attention through some of the play.	Students held the audience's attention throughout the play.	Students captivated the audience at all times.
			Total:	

Applying the Strategy

Playlets and Puppetry can be used in any content area. Students can write and perform scripts to explain the angle measurements in math. They can write scripts to show ways to use vocabulary in context in language arts. In science, puppets can explain how cells move across membranes. Scripts can also be a retelling of an event from history.

Total Physical Response

Total Physical Response (TPR), or more commonly known as Body Mnemonics, is a strategy originally used with second-language learners to make the connection between speech and action; however, with our current understanding of moving information from short term to long term memory, this strategy is good for all learners. Dr. James Asher (2009) is the developer of TPR and teaches that the more often a memory connection is traced, the stronger that connection will be. Students learn to understand the meaning of words using mimes, pictures, and gestures. The teacher-coach uses auditory instruction combined with physical activity to reinforce the word in context. When students perform the movements, it aids their memories. After repeating what the teacher-coach does over and over, students can then do the movements on their own (even in a different order).

This strategy has many benefits, not just for language learners but also for all students. It is a kinesthetic activity and engages students to connect movements to words. It also aids auditory and visual learners as teacher-coaches call out the word for students to hear and then students see others do the activity. Even if some students struggle remembering at first, they can see others modeling the movement.

How to Do It

First, decide on the content that you need to teach students. Use either vocabulary words, steps in a process, or a new concept. Then, assign natural mimes, gestures, or pictures for each word, step, or concept. Call out the word or step, and then model the mimes, gestures, or pictures you have associated with each word, step, or process. Have students select a word from a grab bag and design their own mime, gesture, or picture. The strategy can be modeled before students begin working. Repeat for the other words, steps, or concepts in the lesson, having students repeat these over and over until they can do them on their own.

Ideas for Assessment

Have students show what they have learned by doing this independently. Watching them mimic the actions along with the words independently the following day, gives you the information necessary to know if you need to review or find another set of movements, or if students have grasped the content fully.

Applying the Strategy

TPR can be used for enforcing vocabulary or certain concept understandings. For example, any new vocabulary that students need to learn can include gestures, movements, or pictures to help aid in the memorization and understanding of these words. A teacher-coach can call out these words and then have students say the word and do the movement associated with that word, too. Students can use their bodies to show the steps in a process like writing expository essays. If a new concept is being taught, such as linear equations or the scientific method, students can use their bodies to show these concepts.

Rapping, Rhyming, and Singing

Rapping, Rhyming, and Singing uses music and rhyme to help students learn. Music has many academic benefits for students. Putting words to rhyme or song helps students learn or remember the content better (Ho, Chan, and Cheung 1998; 2003). Language learners have been shown to grow in their language acquisition when rhymes or songs are included in the lessons (Baker 2011; Catterall, Chapleau, and Iwanga 1998). A teacher-coach can use Rapping, Rhyming, and Singing in any content area where there are facts or information that needs to be learned.

How to Do It

This strategy can be done in two different ways. One way is to obtain songs, rhymes, or raps that are already written to perform as choral readings with a class. There are many free audios on the Internet that a teacher-coach can use, or a teacher-coach can write his or her own for the appropriate content. The following example can be read, rapped, or sung:

Mesopotamia and the Fertile Crescent

Mesopotamia was in the Middle East,
By the rivers of the Tigris and the Euphrates.

It was hot, it was dry, there was lots of sand,
Except the Fertile Crescent, which had farming land.

Now the city of Sumer, many people would enter.
There were so many people, it became a trade center.

There were architects for buildings, and artisans and more.
There were scribes who wrote their writings in cuneiform.

Hammurabi came along, the crime rate slowed.
He described all the laws in Hammurabi's Code.

During a choral reading or singing, all students should have a copy of the words. The entire class can also view the words by using a projector, a document camera, or an interactive whiteboard. Lessons can begin with this strategy to get students excited about what they are going to learn. This strategy also can serve as a review of the material at the end of class. These ideas work particularly well with students of all ages.

Another alternative to this strategy is to have students create their own songs, rhymes, or raps about the content and then have them perform it for the class or other students. Collectively, the class can negotiate the criteria for the rubrics. Using this information, the teacher-coach can review the rubrics with students. For example, a set of instructions could contain information for students on the quality of the rap, song, or rhyme as well as the vocabulary, facts, etc.

You may want students to record their performance instead of performing it live. Set a due date for students and have checkpoints along the way so no one gets behind or procrastinates on the project. On the day of the performance, allow students to evaluate peers based on the negotiated criteria for assessment.

Ideas for Assessment

A point-based rubric for Rapping, Rhyming, and Singing could look like the following example. Negotiable contracting can be done with students to choose these criteria and point values.

Figure 7.3 Sample Rapping, Rhyming, and Singing Rubric	

Criteria	Points
The rap contained *at least* four accurate facts.	
The rap used *at least* four key vocabulary words.	
The rap was *at least* two stanzas long.	
The rap was entertaining and enjoyable.	
Presentation skills engaged the audience.	
Total points:	

Students can write peer reviews of the raps, explaining what they felt was catchy or likeable about each one. These should be very positive in nature. You will need to model this for students and give them a word bank, to give them ideas for writing these reviews. Students can also benefit from reading professional reviews on the songs that they know and like.

Applying the Strategy

This strategy can work well with any content through which students must learn facts. Students can create raps about the human body systems in science or functions in math. They can sing about text features in order to help them better understand nonfiction. Students can perform choral readings about important events from history. Have these rhymes, songs, and raps prepared for younger students, and allow the older students to create their own for class performances.

Gallery Walk, Museum Exhibit, or Fair

A Gallery Walk, Museum Exhibit, or Fair is a set of stations in any given place where students simultaneously present to groups of viewers. The viewers rotate from station to station to hear the presentations given by students. These stations act as a gallery where participants walk around viewing information given by students.

Gallery Walks, Museum Exhibits, or Fairs benefit both viewers and presenters. When students present, their performance reinforces what they have learned while working on their speaking skills and also showcasing their talents. They have the opportunity to show what they know in an active way. Viewers visually learn about the material in each gallery by watching the performer and viewing the other materials on display, such as in a Colonial Fair. These presentations are quick and concise, making the learning experience enjoyable for viewers.

How to Do It

The premise for these presentations begins in class with lessons and sometimes independent study projects. Students have a certain amount of time to gather information and then present it in some way. These presentations can be done in small groups or individually and can include speeches given by "famous individuals," explanations of model displays, poetry readings, demonstrations, historical reenactments, or experiments.

Once students have researched topics and prepared for presentations, set up the Gallery Walk, Museum Exhibit, or Fair as stations. These stations can be down a hallway, in clustered cooperative grouping of desks, or around the edges of a classroom. The stations can include props like computers, televisions, artifacts, or models.

Invite parents, administrators, and other classes to the Gallery Walk. A live audience like this gives students a reason for presenting useful information.

Divide the viewers so that each station on the Gallery Walk, Museum Exhibit, or Fair has viewers and every station is presenting at the same time. Once the presentations are finished, participants can rotate to a new station. We recommend that students move at their own pace. Once the activity has been described in detail to the students, implement negotiable contracting of assessments before embarking on the strategy. See Figure 7.4 for a Gallery Walk.

Figure 7.4 Gallery Walk

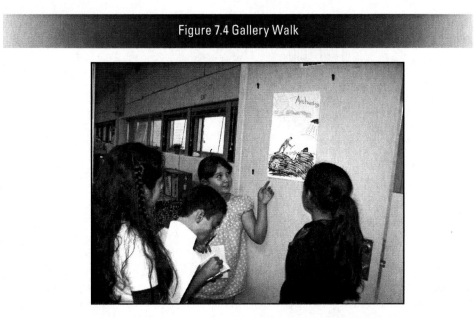

Ideas for Assessment

Student presenters can use questionnaires (two or three yes or no questions), or the students can have brief discussions immediately following their presentations to gain feedback if the information is desired and time is available. This will help students gain the information they need to make improvements the next time this activity is used. We strongly recommend that students fill in a simple chart after viewing each station, demonstrating what they have learned. You can also use a checklist as a grading tool to assess students' information presented in the Gallery Walk, Museum Exhibit, or Fair. See the following sample checklist.

Contents of Math Gallery Walk, Museum Exhibit, or Fair Checklist

❑ stated the problem

❑ showed work

❑ included answer

❑ justified answer

❑ included visual

Applying the Strategy

Gallery Walks, Museum Exhibits, or Fairs are ideal for social studies or language arts where students "become" someone else or they design a fair, such as a Colonial Fair or a Museum Exhibit of Ancient Egypt. They could become a cooper during Colonial Times or Nefertiti from Ancient Egypt. Or they can become different characters from Shakespeare's *A Midsummer Night's Dream* and tell parts of the story from their diverse perspectives. Science Gallery Walks can include showing various parts of a mock crime scene and discussing the evidence, like DNA, chemical analysis, and fingerprints, that is gathered in each part of the scene. In math, give students an open-ended problem to solve, and then have them take turns standing in a Gallery Walk to explain how they solved the problem while small groups rotate around the classroom. This gives students a way to see how a problem can be solved in various ways.

Newscasts, Newspapers, and Slide Show Alive

Perhaps there is no better way to give students real-world experiences in the classroom than having them perform newscasts and write newspaper articles. Both these activities require that students write concise and interesting pieces for others. Newscasts also require that students perform the reading for these pieces, which is good practice for communicating with others. It is obvious that newspaper articles are written to communicate information to others. Newscasts also require a written component that is "acted out" as students present their written articles in a verbal format. Slide Show Alive is where students select images from history and act them out to recreate history. Because of the extra layer of work for students, more time will be needed for Newscasts and Slide Show Alive than for Newspapers.

Many teacher-coaches use this strategy simply for summarizing information students have read. For example, they have students read a text and then create a newscast or newspaper article reporting on the information found in the text. This is a good summarizing activity. However, by just tweaking the activity a little bit, Newscasts, Newspapers, and Slide Show Alive can be used to promote higher-order thinking. For example, when students read a text, have them look for bias in the text. (Many texts have some sort of bias.) Then, have students report on the information from a different viewpoint. In this manner, students have used higher-order thinking as they analyze for bias and then present from different viewpoints, which support the *Common Core State Standards* in the process.

How to Do It

To begin with, students need to view newscasts and newspaper articles as models for their work. Bring in some good models for students to emulate. If possible, find some student newspapers or recorded newscasts to show them, as shown in Figure 7.5.

Figure 7.5 Sample Student Newspaper

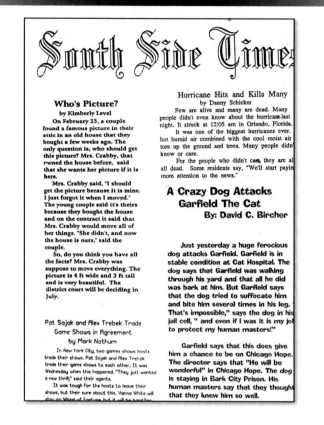

For Newscasts, bring in several clips of professional newscasts, or documents from the History Channel, and have students compare them. Students should look for the difference in the presentation style, types of questions asked, and how the interviews are handled. Give students time to practice a short prewritten script. A few other students can watch and give feedback on the impromptu performances.

For Newspapers, students should be shown different types of articles. They should compare the styles, the written word, and the content. First, model a comparison for the class using a graphic organizer like a Venn diagram or a T-chart. Then, have students work with others to fill out graphic organizers comparing other articles.

Next, students will need to brainstorm ideas for their written or verbal presentations. Decide if students will work on their newspapers and newscasts in small groups (two to four students per group) or individually. If working in a small group, make sure that students know their roles and everyone has a part in writing and presenting. Once the activity has been described in detail, implement negotiable contracting of assessments so that students know what is expected of their news stories and newscasts. Assign a due date, and give students time to work on their stories.

Using the same inquiry skills, students may decide to perform a Slide Show Alive. Students select four to six photographs or paintings from the time period and have them illuminated behind them on an interactive board or from a projector. Then, students act out the photographs in front, using them as "scenes" to make their stories come alive, as they scroll through the set of slides.

Decide ahead of time how students will present the performances. If students are performing live (for Newscasts), set the "stage" for the performances. If students will be reading their articles (Newspapers) in author chairs, prepare students for this oral presentation. For Newscasts and Slide Show Alive, students can make a slide show that is presented behind them while they present their newscasts or depiction of a time period. Give students time to practice for their performances. Once the activity has been described, you may wish to implement negotiable contracting of assessments.

On the day of the performances, have students draw a number that will place them in order of performance. Allow the students to perform their news broadcast stories or share their written newspaper stories. You may wish to film the live performance.

Ideas for Assessment

Allow students to write a brief review of each presentation, stating what they learned and how well it was performed. You may decide to have students share their feelings to help students know how they performed. First, show students what a review looks like so they know what you expect from them. You can provide them with sentence starters or general ideas of things to write. Students will need to know what to focus on before the presentations so that they can take notes. Then, students should use these notes to help them write their reviews.

Applying the Strategy

Students can create Newscasts, Newspapers, and Slide Show Alive to cover important facts in any content area. For example, in math class, a newspaper can cover the ways that angles affect our everyday lives. Science newscasts can highlight what students learn about climate change. For social studies, have students create news stories from ancient times that tell about events and people. Language arts topics can include an event that took place in a book.

Fan Fold Designs

Fan Fold Designs is a hands-on classroom strategy that has students creating contrasting perspectives about an event, a situation, or a thing. It is an unusual opportunity to allow students to work creatively, making a collage or drawing pictures that tell a story from two points of view. Once the collage or pictures are finished, the viewer can see one perspective when standing on the right of a piece. When standing on the left side, the viewer can see the opposite perspective. The example in Figure 7.6 shows two different perspectives of where the people lived. One family lived in the country, and the other family lived in a busy industrial city.

Figure 7.6 Fan Fold Sample

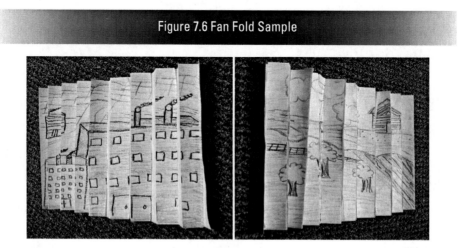

This strategy strengthens students' visual-spatial skills. Those students who are particularly good artists have a chance to show off their skills, but those who are insecure about drawing can still participate because they don't have to draw pictures or scenes. Students can create slogans and banners with key information, and symbols can be created in place of drawn pictures. In fact, students can use pictures from magazines to create collages and thus avoid having to draw at all.

How to Do It

Decide on the topic that students will cover. This activity is best done after students have learned something about the topic. You can have one main topic with many subtopics that fall under it, such as a particular war with the subtopics of leaders, battles, or weapons. Follow the steps in Figure 7.7 to create a Fan Fold Design.

Figure 7.7 Steps to Making a Fan Fold

Step 1
Distribute two sheets of prelined **regular** 8.5" by 11" paper to students. Ask students to flip the paper over so that the lines do not show. The paper should be placed in the landscape position.

Step 2
Using the Venn diagram as a guide, each student creates a contrasting picture using crayons, colored pencils, markers, etc.

Figure 7.7 Steps to Making a Fan Fold *(cont.)*

Step 3
Each student takes the picture that was drawn and flips it over so that the lines are visible.

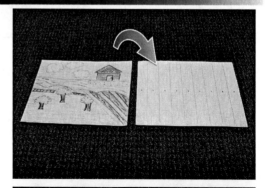

Step 4
Cut the paper along the lines. Place the strips in order and put them aside.

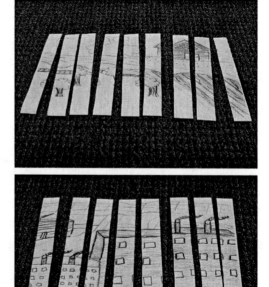

Figure 7.7 Steps to Making a Fan Fold *(cont.)*

Step 5
Distribute two sheets of prelined 8.5" by 11" **cardstock** paper to students.

Step 6
Fold each cardstock along the lines into a fan.

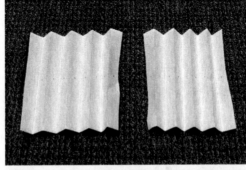

Step 7
Tape them together and flip them over so that the numbers and lines do not show, making one large fan. This should be done prior to pasting the strips of paper on the fan.

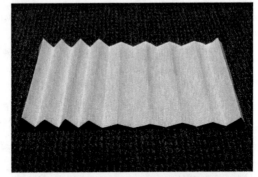

Step 8
Take the first set of strips and, in order, place them on the left side of each fold.

Figure 7.7 Steps to Making a Fan Fold *(cont.)*

Step 9

Check to make sure that the picture works by placing yourself at an angle to view the picture. If the picture looks correct, glue the rest of them down, making sure that the forward edge of each strip lines up with the front fold in the fan.

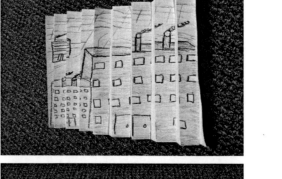

Step 10

Take the second set of strips and place them on the right side of each fold.

Step 11

Check to make sure that the second picture works by placing yourself at an angle to view the picture. If the picture looks correct, glue the rest of them down, making sure that the forward edge of each strip lines up with the fold in the fan.

Once the Fan Fold Design has been created, have each student write a paragraph description of his or her viewpoint. The paragraph should explain what is in the image, and why. Students should share their pictures and paragraphs with the class. It is imperative to show students a model before embarking on this activity. Once they have a clear understanding of the task, utilize negotiable contracting of assessment to design rubrics. Criteria may include, but not be limited to:

- Two contrasting pictures are displayed.
- Pictures present excellent detail.
- Includes good artistic layout and design.
- Paragraphs are written clearly.
- Paragraphs are written clearly.
- Venn diagram displays the common and opposing points.

Ideas for Assessment

Student pictures should clearly show one of two viewpoints. Give students a checklist of items you want to see in their pictures, such as slogans, images, scenes, words, and icons. You can assess the content of their pictures according to the checklists. You can also assess student understanding as students share their Fan Fold Designs and what their pictures symbolize, using a rating chart like the one in Figure 7.8. Assign point values to each criterion.

Figure 7.8 Sample Fan Fold Rubric

Criteria	Novice	Apprentice	Proficient	Distinguished
Picture Viewpoints	Two distinct viewpoints were not made or hardly noticeable as a comparison.	Two distinct viewpoints were marginally made or hardly noticeable as a comparison.	Two distinct viewpoints were clearly made.	Two distinct viewpoints were compared and contrasted with great detail.
Paragraphs	Paragraphs were difficult to understand.	Paragraphs were marginally clear.	Paragraphs were understandable.	Paragraphs were clear and easy to understand.

Applying the Strategy

Any time there are at least two opposing viewpoints, Fan Fold Designs is a great visual way to have students express those viewpoints. Fan Fold Designs can be used to show how characters view events differently in a novel. They can show how different people view events from history. They can also display the difference between two-dimensional and three-dimensional drawings in math, or they can compare two different animals in the animal kingdom in science.

Molding Dough Sculptures

In this strategy, adapted from Linda Schwartz Green and Diane Casale-Giannola's Play Dough Construction, the teacher-coach calls out a topic and students create sculptures to show what they know or have learned. It ends with a student explanation of their sculpture, showing how it relates to the content.

Students who need multisensory strategies benefit from this activity because they are using their hands to create something meaningful. Kinesthetic learners need movement that is involved with this activity to keep them engaged and learning. Movement for these types of learners is a natural way of transferring learning from abstract to concrete (Jackson 2009). Nonreaders benefit from this activity, and the teacher-coach can see if they comprehend information from their lessons. This type of activity takes away the worry and stress connected with reading and writing words from these students so that they can show what they know visually. And for those students who don't excel in visual arts, it provides new outlets for them to explore and practice.

How to Do It

Begin with a review of the concepts so that students can activate their prior knowledge. This activity can take place at the beginning, middle, or end of a lesson.

Give students paper plates to serve as a work surface. Distribute molding dough or clay to your students. You can make your own dough using the following ingredients:

$\frac{1}{4}$ cup salt

1 cup flour

$\frac{1}{4}$ cup water

Tell students to create something, using their molding dough, that represents a certain concept, for example, the letter *W* or a symbol that represents a nation, the beginning sound of the word *dinosaur*, or a symbol that represents the character in the book you just read as a class. Give students a few minutes to create their Molding Dough Sculptures. See Figure 7.9 for an example of a Molding Dough Sculpture.

Figure 7.9 Sample Molding Dough Sculpture

Ideas for Assessment

Allow each student to share with you, share with partners sitting nearby, or share with the class. This is where the teacher-coach can check for student understanding. If time permits, allow students to repeat this activity to show what they know about more concepts.

Applying the Strategy

This strategy works well with letter sounds, spelling, things a book character would use, numbers, symbols, and equations. In a very basic sense for kinesthetic reasons or just to switch up the monotony of the routine, students can use the dough to spell out words or mathematical symbols. To be used creatively, ask students to create something new to symbolize what they have read or what they understand about the content. You might also want students to practice their visualization skills by showing concretely what they see in their minds after reading a text. Be sure to check for student understanding to get the most from using this strategy.

Conclusion

The strategies in this chapter promote creative and dramatic arts and include Playlets and Puppetry, Total Physical Response, Rapping, Rhyming, and Singing, Gallery Walk, Newscasts and Newspapers, Fan Fold Designs, and Molding Dough Sculptures. Creative and dramatic arts contain numerous skills that can be strengthened in students by using these strategies. Students will become better public speakers, actors, and writers as a result of these activities. They have the chance to learn kinesthetically and visually in many of these examples. Best of all, they get to apply what they have learned about a topic in a creative manner.

Let's Think and Discuss

1. Describe in detail which strategies in this chapter would be a good fit for your students, and why.

2. Explain specifically for what content Fan Fold Designs can be used in your classroom.

3. In what ways could you work with students who seem reluctant at first to try to produce something creative?

Chapter

Inquiry Learning Strategies

Inquiry is a natural instinct, and it's at the very heart of learning. To inquire is to seek information and ask questions. No matter the age, people inquire about their surroundings. They investigate. They wonder. They experiment.

The idea of inquiry-based learning began long ago, with Socrates. Socrates asked his students many questions but gave few answers. He wanted his students to wonder and discover knowledge for themselves. During the 1930s, John Dewey did the same. In the 1960s, Richard Suchman pioneered an inquiry-based teaching program. He believed that inquiry was something a person did when left alone to learn.

An inquiry-based classroom is quite different from the typical class where the teacher transmits all knowledge to the students. Real inquiry-based learning has students asking questions, gathering data, and implementing information that leads to new knowledge because the foundation of inquiry-based learning is student involvement. When teacher-coaches spark curiosity in students, they learn how to identify problems, reflect, ask questions, and pose theories. Students learn the various coaching strategies such as GOPER Model of Accountable Talk. Through this process, students actively form their own knowledge.

Inquiry-based learning is important for several reasons. Employers today search for problem solvers who not only know how to ask the right questions but also can gather the data and then convert it to useful information to help companies grow. Inquiry-based learning trains students to be problem solvers for life because they learn to transfer the new knowledge to new situations to solve more problems (Bransford et al. 1986). Second, inquiry-based learning nurtures the desire to know about our world. There is an endless amount of information to learn about the world in which we live, and as society and Earth change, there will be more to know. If students do not become lifelong learners, then who will transmit knowledge in the future?

The inquiry learning strategies discussed in this chapter include:

- The 5E Model (page 162)
- Project-Based Learning (page 165)
- Research and Investigations (page 168)
- Problem-Based Learning (page 172)
- Creative Problem Solving (page 176)
- Discovery Learning (page 179)
- Scavenger Hunt (page 182)
- Interviewing for Intention (page 186)

The 5E Model

The Biological Science Curriculum Study (BSCS 2006), a team led by principal investigator Roger Bybee, developed the instructional model for constructivism, called the "Five Es." This model employs the 5 Es—Engage, Explore, Explain, Elaborate, and Evaluate—and is based on a constructivist philosophy of learning. Constructivists believe that students build or construct their own understanding of new ideas based on what they already know. Each *E* represents part of a sequential instructional process or learning cycle designed to help students construct their own learning experiences and ultimate understanding of the topic or concept.

At the *Engage* stage, teacher-coaches introduce a topic or concept with an intriguing, fascinating, or challenging question or demonstration designed to capture students' interest, curiosity, and attention. At this stage, teacher-coaches do not seek a "right answer." Instead, they prompt students to talk about what they already know about the topic (or think they may know) and discuss what else students would like to know.

During *Exploration*, students conduct various hands-on or problem-solving activities designed to help them explore the topic and make connections to related concepts, often within groups or teams. During this stage, students share common experiences while the teacher acts as an instructional coach or teacher-coach, providing or aiding students to find materials as needed and guiding the students' focus.

At the *Explain* stage, teacher-coaches help students observe patterns, analyze results, and/or draw conclusions based on their activities and investigations. Teacher-coaches also encourage students to define relevant vocabulary.

In the *Elaborate* stage, students build on the concepts or ideas they have learned and make connections to other related concepts and new situations.

In the final stage, teacher-coaches *Evaluate*, or assess, students' understanding of the topic studied and may encourage peer assessment. This evaluation can be formal or informal but should demonstrate a clear understanding of what students have learned throughout the course of the lesson.

How to Do It

Figure 8.1 shows how the 5E Model allows for fluid assessment and re-teaching opportunities. Each lesson begins with an *Engaging* activity that grabs the students' attention. The *Explore* section of the lesson involves students exploring the concept either on their own or with some teacher-coach guidance. Once explorations of the concept are complete, explain the concept and discuss it with the students. Here, informally assess whether students are beginning to understand that concept. If they are not, students should spend more time exploring the concept. If students understand the concept, move to the *Elaborate* section of the lesson. Students make connections to other scientific concepts and extend what they have learned. If students are having difficulties with this part of the lesson, spend more time explaining and allowing students to further explore the concept before moving back to the *Elaborate* section. Finally, when students are successfully making connections and extending the concept, they can be formally *Evaluated* on their knowledge.

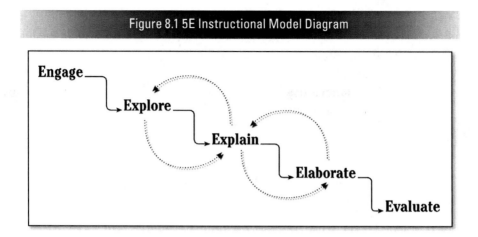

Figure 8.1 5E Instructional Model Diagram

Engage
Explore
Explain
Elaborate
Evaluate

Ideas for Assessment

As previously mentioned, student understanding is assessed during the final stage of *Evaluate*, but informal formative assessments take place throughout this model. A teacher-coach might want to perform a formal evaluation in the form of a quiz or a test, or the evaluation can be informal by having students verbally explain what they know or simply observing students as they are working through an activity. As in other strategies found throughout this book, the teacher should negotiably contract the assessment with the students ahead of time. With a project like this, we encourage teachers to use a rubric.

Applying the Strategy

While the 5E Model can be used in other content areas as a way to design a strong lesson, it is most commonly used with science curriculum. For example, in a lesson about force, students are first engaged in considering how to elevate a heavy object, using only paper. Next, students explore how to change the speed, direction, and shape of four other objects. Then, the teacher-coach explains different kinds of forces and how they are measured. Students learn and elaborate on how forces, not engines or motors, act to keep a roller coaster in motion. Finally, students examine the essential question of the lesson and are evaluated on what they have learned.

Project-Based Learning

At its very core, Project-Based Learning engages students with content while having them produce projects to show what they have learned. It is an avenue by which students "do something" instead of "learn about something." Most importantly, Project-Based Learning replaces the use of ineffective activity sheets and utilizes higher-order thinking skills.

According to Larmer and Mergendoller (2010), meaningful projects fit two criteria: the work must be personally meaningful, and the work should fulfill an educational purpose. But, does merely researching a topic and creating a display of some sort—web page, yard sign, or postcard—ensure that the assignment tapped into students' higher-order thinking skills? Not necessarily. Creating projects that tap into students' higher-order thinking takes purposeful planning.

Larmer and Mergendoller (2010) propose several key components of a good project. The first is an engaging entry point to the topic. This engaging experience can be a video, a discussion, a guest speaker, a field trip, or a scenario, just to name a few ideas. The goal is to get students to care about the topic and personally accept the challenge of the assignment. Second, there should be a driving question that frames the project. Examples might include concrete questions (*Was being an explorer in the 1400–1500s a good profession?*), abstract questions (*If you were to design a bridge for a local waterway, describe your choice of construction [post and lintel, arched, or suspension] that you would consider?*), or problem-solving questions (*What can we do to make math class more interesting?*). Whatever the question is, it should drive to the goal of what you want students to learn while doing their projects. Finally, students should be given choices when it comes to working on projects. Giving students choices results in better completed work because they feel ownership in making their own decisions. Project-Based Learning activities are perfect for this reason because they are learner-centered, giving students control over what they will be producing.

One benefit of Project-Based Learning is that the time devoted to it can be very flexible. Teacher-coaches can decide the length of an activity. To shorten the time frame, teacher-coaches need to offer project choices that can be completed within a short amount of time. Instead of assigning a wiki page (which would take longer), assign a trading card, which can be done in a shorter amount of time. However, higher-order thinking activities should be part of the assigned projects. Students can create a trading card to show what they know about a person, a place, or a thing that they have been studying while adding in a component such as predicting what is coming next for that person, place, or thing on the trading card.

When applicable to the projects, Project-Based Learning can help to develop valuable research skills. Project-Based Learning activities can provide students the opportunity to learn how to research topics and then put what they know into unique and creative products. Project-Based Learning provides students the opportunity to work in groups or individually. Teacher-coaches should use checkpoints to help students successfully complete the projects on time and teach time management.

These projects provide concrete assessment pieces because they show how students apply what they learn, yet each one is in a unique, creative format. Teacher-coaches can use them in portfolios or as a grade. Let students explain their thinking behind the projects and offer grades according to what you see, and what is explained to you. This way, students are assessed on knowledge that is gained by doing the projects.

How to Do It

To begin, decide on the driving question that will frame the projects. Remember, these can be concrete, abstract, or problem-solving questions. Then, decide how much time should be devoted to this activity. Will it be a small amount of time (one class period) or a few weeks? A shorter time frame is suggested for younger students. Based on the time frame, decide on the project selections from which students can choose. These projects should be completed within the time frame you allowed. If the project is set for a longer time frame, set checkpoints to keep students on task and accountable for their work. Use an Excel spreadsheet, Trello on the web, or a paper checklist to keep track of these checkpoints. If used effectively, Project-Based Learning will train your students to manage their time, use their creativity, and learn important content.

Ideas for Assessment

When assessing projects, it is best to be as objective as possible. Trying to assess whether student work is creative might be too subjective. Instead, look for objective things that can be assessed. When designing a rubric, negotiating the criteria for assessments is crucial in trying to create student ownership. First, have students think about what it is that you are trying to assess. What are the most important things? The project should show that students understand the concepts that were taught. You can also look at the facts, vocabulary, and images included in the projects. If these things were included and used accurately, then points can be assigned. A point-based rubric might look similar to Figure 8.2. The criteria and point values may be determined during negotiable contracting.

Figure 8.2 Project-Based Learning Rubric

Criteria	Points
The project shows student understanding of the concepts.	
Four vocabulary words were included and used accurately.	
Four facts were included.	
The project was turned in on time.	
The project engages the viewer or reader.	
The project is exciting to the audience.	
Total	

Applying the Strategy

Project-Based Learning can be used in any content area. For example, in science, students can learn about genetics and take on a film project that exemplifies what they learn. In math, students can create social media web pages that show how professionals use fractions on a daily basis. In language arts, students can create creatures using various craft supplies and then produce a how-to guide about it to share. In social studies, students can create diaries from people in the past in the style of Jeff Kinney's *Diary of a Wimpy Kid* series.

Research and Investigations

This strategy gives students practice with performing research on a topic. Knowing how to research and investigate topics is something that will benefit students throughout their lives. In order to find information in the most efficient ways, students should learn proper methods for researching and investigating a topic. Never before have there been more ways to access information. Traditional print information is still available as well as newer ways to research using technology. But even with the use of technology, the art of learning good research practices retains key elements that students still need. For example, even though much research can be conducted online, sources still need to be cited properly and vetted for reliability. Students still need to learn the most efficient ways to research. When performing research online, what are the key words that will bring up the most important information? These skills can be taught even to young students. Each year, teacher-coaches can build upon these skills.

The more time that we spend researching, the better we get at it. For this reason, it is important that students learn to research at a young age. Begin with topics they enjoy, such as animals. Have them select an animal that would make an unusual pet and then perform research to find out more about it. The key with young students is to have substantial amounts of materials for them to use while researching. Books and websites need to be appropriate for their reading levels. Give them the structure of things to find out. They can show their work on a display board like the one in Figure 8.3.

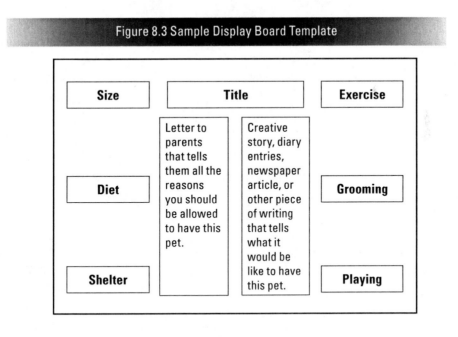

Figure 8.3 Sample Display Board Template

How to Do It

To begin, select a topic that supports a grade-level objective that lends itself to research and investigation. As always, find a way to make it interesting to students. This can be in the form of a question that hooks students to the topic or a mystery that students need to solve, for example, *What really happened to Amelia Earhart?* This gives students a reason and desire for research. You can place students into small groups for collaboration and brainstorming about the topic or do it as a whole-class activity.

Next, present students with grade-level appropriate materials for research. Bookmark websites, books, magazine articles, and other materials for students to use to gain the information they need. Encourage students to bring in materials on their own.

At first, students will need you to model and explain how to research. For example, a teacher-coach will need to show students how to do an Internet search and properly record the information by citing a reliable website. Show students how to carefully paraphrase information without plagiarizing it. Then, show how to look at the index or table of contents in the book to find a topic to read instead of reading the entire book. In this way, a teacher-coach is showing how to perform smart research without wasting a lot of time reading information that won't pertain to the topic. Show students how to cite the references using a particular format. Depending on their backgrounds, some students might need extra help in this area. It is often beneficial if students have a guide as they begin researching. Students and the teacher-coach collectively brainstorm a set of questions to help guide their research in the right direction.

Set a due date for the research to be completed, and then decide on a way for students to show what they have learned from their research. This can be in the form of a project, a paper, a poster, a display, a demonstration, or a multi-media presentation. Before beginning to prepare for the project, students will need to know their projects' assessment criteria. Once the assignment has been described in detail, implement negotiable contracting of assessments. Discuss this information with students and allow them to present their projects to the class.

Ideas for Assessment

As mentioned with project-based assignments, you can assess student work on their final creations by looking for how the project shows student understanding of the topic. You can also assess students by the process of their research. For example, the following rubric assesses how well students performed their research and the materials they used for their research.

Figure 8.4 Sample Research and Investigation Rubric

Research and Investigation Rubric			
Novice	**Apprentice**	**Proficient**	**Distinguished**
Students did not collect any research notes.	Students collected some research notes but not two pages.	Students collected nearly all two pages of research notes.	Students collected at least two pages of research notes.
None of the research notes are relevant.	Some of the research notes are relevant.	Nearly all of the research notes are relevant to the topic.	The research notes are relevant to the topic.
Students did not include proper citations.	Students included some proper citations.	Students properly cited nearly all sources.	Students included proper citations.
Students did not use any sources for research.	Students used fewer than four sources for research.	Students used nearly all four sources for research.	Students used at least, if not more than, four sources for research.
Total Score:			

Applying the Strategy

Students can research the technology used during the Crusades in a history class and then create a mock tool kit for a soldier back then. For science, students can work together to write an illustrated mini-encyclopedia of snakes found in the region where they live. Students can research famous authors and make documentaries about the person. For math, students can research interest rates for investing in stocks, CDs, and traditional savings accounts and make a brochure that shows all three with recommendations.

Problem-Based Learning

Problem-Based Learning is a problem-solving strategy that engages students in solving a lifelike or real-life problem. This strategy gives students the opportunity to collaborate with their classmates as they study the issues of a certain problem. Students can use information they find through research to synthesize viable solutions. The amount of direct instruction in a problem-based classroom is very limited, so students have to take on the responsibility for their own learning. The teacher's role is much like that of a coach. The teacher-coach presents the problematic situation, acts as a resource guide or consultant, and serves as a co-investigator who keeps students on task. The teacher-coach prompts students and ask questions like *How do you know this to be true? Tell me more about that. Let's examine what you found that supports what you are saying.* He or she poses questions that allow students to question their logic in a nonthreatening manner. These gentle inquiries serve as role models so that students can ask similar questions to their peers. The student's role is that of a participant who grapples with the complexity of the situation while investigating and resolving the problem from the inside out.

There are many reasons for using Problem-Based Learning with students. First, we know that our minds are capable of thinking through complex situations, which promotes higher-level thinking skills. Research says that it is the complex challenges that develop our intellect and ability to think productively (Caine and Caine 1997; Diamond and Hopson 1998). These types of problems do not provide just one right answer. Students are forced into thinking both critically and creatively as they seek to find solutions to problems.

Problem-Based Learning also increases motivation in students. Recently, some professors at the college level have begun to restructure their course work around Problem-Based Learning. They do this by taking the final exam and working backwards to structure the course around a problem that teaches the key concepts they want their students to learn. Students see that the outcome of their work can make a real difference in society.

This type of learning provides opportunities for students to work with others, listen to one another, and synthesize information. While collaborating, great ideas can flow freely. Brainstorming with others brings out creative ideas that might not have been evident if students had been working alone. Problem-Based Learning is continuous brainstorming of what the problem is and how it can be solved.

This strategy also provides students the chance to develop strong work ethics. So much work, energy, and thinking go into solving problems. Strategies are generated for identifying and defining the problem, gathering information, analyzing data, and building and testing the hypothesis.

Finally, Problem-Based Learning is active. As students struggle to figure out a problem and apply what they are learning, they are more likely to remember the key concepts taught in that lesson.

How to Do It

A typical Problem-Based Learning lesson has several cycles. These steps can be repeated as many times as necessary to come to a conclusion. First, locate a real-world problem that connects to your learning standards and goals. Determine facts and find a way for students to enter the problem. Tie it to something that they are interested in. This is called the *hook*.

After you present the problem, students discuss what they know to be the facts of the problem. They can use a graphic organizer to keep track of this information. Have students analyze the problem, brainstorm ideas about the problem, and create an exact statement of the problem. This is the *hypothesis*. The problem statement might sound like this: *How can we...in such a way that...?*

Tell students that they need to identify information necessary to understand the problem and identify resources to be used to gather information. Students can find and share information by interviewing, collecting data, and conducting other forms of research. They can revise the problem statement and ask additional questions if necessary. Ask students to develop solutions by studying the information and finding a solution that fits best as well as considering the consequences for their solution. Students can develop a presentation in which they explain, apply, and justify their solution to the problem. You may wish to implement negotiable contracting of assessments so that students are familiar with the assignment expectations.

Ideas for Assessment

Students can be assessed on a number of things in Problem-Based Learning. You can assess them on the process of their investigations, including how they interview, collect data, and conduct and include other forms of research. If students produce a product, its components can be assessed. Another idea is to assess their final presentations that explain both of these as well as their final solutions. The assessment can include both the mechanics and the content of their presentations in the form of a checklist.

Presentation Checklist Assessment

- The student made eye contact.

- The student spoke loudly enough for the audience to hear.

- Content was relevant and resourceful.

- Research was thorough, and citations were given.

- The reader or performer engaged the audience.

- The presentation was interesting and insightful.

Notes about the presentation: _____

Applying the Strategy

This strategy can be used in any content area. Teacher-coaches can design a Problem-Based Learning activity around a historical problem such as the Japanese internment camps during WWII and decide if the Bill of Rights applies at all times, or they can investigate a mystery from history, such as what became of the lost colony of Roanoke. After the solutions are found, students can compare to show how the problem was solved in the past. For language arts, students can consider if classics should still be read as a requirement in the classroom or discuss the controversy between eBooks and paper books. A science example could focus on the drought found in a particular region. Students can also consider where to rebuild after a hurricane if the dunes have moved inland. In math, students can consider what would be the repercussions if we used a different base number system, such as a base 12 or base 8.

Creative Problem Solving

Creative Problem Solving (CPS) is a problem-solving strategy that traditionally uses six steps to solve a problem (Osborn 1993; Treffinger, Isaken, and Stead-Dorval 2006).

1. Locate a problem.

2. Find out the details about it.

3. Define it.

4. Brainstorm ideas.

5. Evaluate the ideas.

6. Implement the solution to see if it works.

Many of the benefits and reasons for using CPS are related to promoting higher-order thinking skills because the problems are open-ended. Students think both critically and creatively as they seek to find solutions to problems. CPS gives students a reason to be challenged and keeps them from jumping rashly to conclusions. The end result of completing something that was first perceived as difficult builds confidence for future challenging tasks. This type of learning provides opportunities for students to work with others in collaborative groups. Finally, the strategies that students use in CPS will benefit them their entire lives. CPS gives students the opportunity to build "creative muscles." The more a student practices creativity, the stronger those creative muscles will be. CPS and Problem-Based Learning are similar, but while Project-Based Learning focuses on learning content through a problem, CPS focuses on finding creative solutions to a problem.

How to Do It

Traditionally, CPS has used six steps to solve problems. The first step is *mess finding*, which is the act of locating a problem for students to solve. Next, *fact finding* is the step at which students examine details and list all facts known about a problem. *Problem finding* involves students looking for alternative ways to define the problem, using this sentence starter: *In what ways might we...?* During *idea finding*, students brainstorm in hopes of finding solutions. *Solution finding* is the evaluation of their ideas produced from brainstorming. Finally, *acceptance finding* is the stage at which students implement the solution to see if it works.

To make this easier to understand, these six steps can be simplified into three main steps: (1) understanding the problem, (2) generating ideas, and (3) planning for action.

1. **Understanding the problem** can include first finding the problem and then finding out all the facts about that problem. It can take a considerable amount of time for research and analysis to really know what the problem is all about. This step includes mess finding, fact finding, and problem finding.

2. **Generating ideas** is the brainstorming part of Creative Problem Solving. Students try to think of many varied possible solutions to the problem. Students write down all ideas and take each one seriously. Often, some very unusual solutions are proposed. Sometimes, these end up being the best solutions, so they should never be discarded early on in the brainstorming process. This step, called *idea finding*, should be free of evaluation or criticism.

3. **Planning for action** is when a solution to the problem is decided upon and implemented. After students have let the ideas settle, the ones from the previous step can be criticized and evaluated. To narrow down ideas, students can list what is good and what is bad about each of their ideas. This makes students analyze their ideas and think through them. Solution finding and acceptance finding are included in this third step.

These steps can be divided into three days but a good teacher will modify the schedule according to the needs of the students:

- Day 1—Students must understand the problem.
- Day 2—Students can generate ideas.
- Day 3—Students can make a plan for what they would do.

Be prepared to lead students through the steps of Creative Problem Solving the first few times this strategy is implemented. In a classroom, students can work with their classmates to find solutions to problems. Teacher-coaches can facilitate small-group discussions and brainstorming sessions with students. By modeling and coaching them through CPS, students learn how to take responsibility for their own learning. Your role is much like a coach in the sense that you keep students on task and help them to find the problem and generate many possible solutions.

As a teacher-coach, you can employ the GOPER model in tandem with Creative Problem Solving to support your students as they work. For detailed information on how to implement the step, please see Chapter One.

Ideas for Assessment

Use both formative and summative assessments in classroom discussions and journal writing. Students can write in their journals before they start the problem; in this way, they are predicting. They can also write during the problem solving, so that their thinking process is shown. Students should also write after they have solved the problem to show how they came up with their final solution. A final project can sum up their learning. Use one of the previously mentioned rubrics for the projects.

Applying the Strategy

Every content area can have scenarios with problems for students to solve. Language arts examples include ways to help welcome language learners at your school. Science examples can include removing an animal from an ecosystem to study the effects on it. Social studies students can design their own culture and decide where it will fit in with today's world. In math, students can be challenged to measure without using standard units. A teacher-coach might ask students how they can measure the length of a desk and still make sure that everyone understands what their form of measurement means.

Discovery Learning

Discovery Learning is an inquiry-based learning method. It takes place when a teacher-coach facilitates an experiment, acts as a coach, and provides clues along the way to help students arrive at solutions. In this way, teacher-coaches provide students with certain tools for learning a concept, and the students make sense of the tools. Discovery Learning has historically been more of a teacher-centered strategy than a student-centered strategy. However, it can be a good starting point to get students on their way to becoming independent thinkers. We recommend that teachers today be cognizant that students have to construct knowledge rather than be told. We included Bruner as a historical base.

Benefits of Discovery Learning include students having a role in their own learning and developing their creativity as they work on problems. Students develop problem-solving strategies when they encounter unfamiliar territory. Discovery Learning is used mostly while students problem-solve. It produces students who are constructivists as they work with others and learn from firsthand experiences. New information and skills are discovered as students use prior knowledge and past experiences. Students find problems, gather information, develop hypotheses, and prove their solutions.

Discovery Learning is largely attributed to Jerome Bruner. During the 1960s and 1970s, Bruner worked with the National Science Foundation, developing science curriculum. It was his beliefs that led to the promotion of discovery learning. Bruner believed science curriculum should help students to become problem solvers by using discovery and inquiry. He said real learning takes place when students become problem solvers. As students test hypotheses and develop generalizations, they interact with the environment around them and discover solutions. When they discover their own solutions, they better remember what was taught (Bruner 2004).

Bruner went against the thought that science was merely the accumulation of wisdom from textbooks. He believed knowing was a process. When students are given structured problems, they learn concepts and problem-solving skills. The desire to know motivates students to solve the problems. Bruner's theory of instruction has four parts:

1. Curiosity and uncertainty

2. Structure of knowledge

3. Sequencing

4. Motivation

Curiosity and Uncertainty—The first part of Bruner's theory was that classes should facilitate experiences to make students want to learn or be predisposed to learning. The problem being explored must offer alternative solutions. This experience must have an amount of uncertainty, which in turn would pique students' interest and curiosity to solve the problem.

Structure of Knowledge—Bruner's second (and some say the most important) point states that the teacher "must specify the ways in which a body of knowledge should be structured so that it can be most readily grasped" by students (Bruner 2004). He believed that teachers could present any problem to students as long as they simplify it, so students can understand it. Whether the topic is chemistry or physics or the concept is atomic structure or Newton's laws, Bruner thought it could be taught to any level of students. To do this, it must be represented by either enactive representation (a set of actions), iconic representation (a set of pictures), or symbolic representation (logical statements).

Sequencing—Bruner's third principle states that the learner should be led through content sequentially. This will help students understand and transfer the knowledge that is learned. First, students should complete hands-on activities that are concrete. Next, they should have a visual representation of the concept. Finally, students should move to using vocabulary or symbols having to do with the concept. He notes that this progression depends on individual learning styles.

Motivation—Bruner's final principle is that rewards from the teacher should gradually decrease until students are wholly satisfied with their inward abilities to solve problems. It is important that students receive feedback so that they can develop knowledge and understanding.

How to Do It

Begin a Discovery Learning lesson by having students choose a scenario, a problem, or data to analyze. Distribute copies of the task to students. The task guides students where to begin and what to do, but it does not give students the answers or tell them the meaning of their investigations. The goal is for students to discover it themselves. Work with students to negotiate the task criteria. Students may determine that the task should be to examine the family tree of a fictitious family and tell about what they notice. By looking at this data, the end result would be students discovering the harmful diseases that have been passed on to children. Students read through the task and answer questions. Provide students time to work on the problem. Students work together to create guided questions to keep them on track. In the end, students should present their findings to the class or in small groups. End with a whole-class discussion about what they found.

Ideas for Assessment

Assessment for Discovery Learning can be based on the negotiated criteria, which may include student presentations, student projects (if assigned), or the process of solving the problem. If focusing on the process, formative assessment must be used to keep track of how students discover knowledge. To do this, have students write in a daily journal explaining their steps and thought processes along the way. They can draw pictures in these journals. At the end, you will have a collection of their thoughts as they worked.

Applying the Strategy

Discovery Learning can work with any content area but works particularly well with science topics. Any kind of experiment that students conduct is a perfect venue for discovering the key concepts. Students can reflect on their findings and discover what the teacher desired them to know. Students can discover what polygons are by observing different kinds of shapes and categorizing them into two groups. A language arts class can have students discover that the Latin and Greek roots of words will help them construct meaning of new and unfamiliar vocabulary. A social studies lesson might have students "reliving" an event from history and observe the unfairness of that event.

Scavenger Hunt

The Scavenger Hunt strategy is always fun and can be educational at the same time. Many museums throughout the country now have Scavenger Hunts for children and adults alike. This strategy can be utilized by setting up a museum exhibit in the classroom filled with pictures that do not have any identification, or it can be used to have students locate information through their own research, which is then placed in a booklet.

How to Do It

Brainstorm with students what kinds of things help us learn about the past, especially during ancient times when written records were scarce. Students may list written records, statues, pottery, tombs, furniture, artifacts, and even garbage as items used to learn about the past. Once students have brainstormed a list of items, ask them to find an image or a replica of an object for the classroom museum.

Museum Exhibit

Students should conduct research on the image and write a short description for it. The completed descriptions will be photocopied and numbered from 1 to 26. Laminate and post pictures around the classroom, making it into a mock museum. Be certain to assign a letter to each picture (A-Z).

Pair up students on the day of the hunt. Have students match each description to one of the museum pieces. Note that it is important to assign a letter to all laminated pictures and assign a number to each of the descriptions. For each correct match made, a point will be assigned. A pair of students may not agree with a choice, but if this happens, the person who gets the correct answer receives an additional point. Depending on the number of pieces in the museum, the Scavenger Hunt will be played in chunks or sets. After each set, students can take a review break. Each person silently selects a museum piece and acts it out for his or her team. The team must guess the piece before continuing through to the end of the game. This is a nice way of infusing body mnemonics.

After describing this strategy to students and before they embark on the task, participate in negotiable contracting of assessments. If they were the teacher, what would they look for to see the highest quality work? Criteria may include but are not limited to the following:

- Is the description written with clarity?

- Does the description give enough detail that would interest the reader?

- How well are you and your partner working together while trying to match the pictures to the descriptions during the hunt at the Museum Exhibit?

  - Did you give each other eye contact?

  - Did you listen and respond to one another?

  - Did you move from piece to piece in a timely manner?

Booklet

Another way of designing the Scavenger Hunt strategy is by having students gather information that relates to a particular discipline. For example, they may gather information on all of the levels of government, such as local, state, and federal. Students piece together this information in booklet form. Explain to students that even though they will be working as a pair, each member must make his or her own copy by hand or in digital format. They should be given one or two days before the due date to share information with one another.

If the study of government was the topic, the following questions could be posed to have students inquire about the House of Representatives.

- What determines the number of members in the House of Representatives?

- What is the term of office for a representative, and how often are elections held?

- In which congressional district do you live?

- What is the name of the person who represents your district in the House of Representatives? Write down the office telephone number of your representative and the address of his or her local office in your community.

As a teacher-coach, begin the negotiable contracting of assessment with students before they embark on the task. What do they think will be expected of them while they construct their own booklets? Explain that these items will determine the criteria for their grade. Criteria may include but are not limited to:

- Are all the questions answered?

- Are the descriptions written with clarity?

- Does the description give enough detail that would interest the reader?

- Did the researcher add interesting material, such as pictures, video clips, or artifacts?

- Was care given to the artistic layout and design of the overall booklet?

Ideas for Assessment

As part of formative assessment, each of these strategies require a different form of assessment.

Museum Exhibit:

In this case, the criteria that was established ahead of time, is used during performance assessment in a chart. Students' names are written on the left side of a grid and the criteria established ahead of time is written on the top. The teacher-coach roams the room and gives each student a ✓–, ✓, ✓+, or ✓++. The teacher-coach can also assign numbers from 1–4. Examples for both types of performance assessments are shown below.

Museum Exhibit

	Clarity of Writing	Depth to Make it Interesting	Eye Contact	Listens Well	Responds Appropriately
Mitchell	3	3	4	4	3
Francois	3	2	3	3	3
Martina	4	4	4	3	4
Sasha	2	3	4	4	3

Scavenger Hunt Journal

	Clarity of Writing	Depth to Make it Interesting	All Questions Answered	Insertions of Pictures, Video Clips or Artifacts	Artistic Design and Layout
Mitchell	✓	✓–	✓	✓+	✓+
Francois	✓–	✓+	✓	✓	✓++
Martina	✓+	✓+	✓–	✓	✓
Sasha	✓++	✓	✓++	✓–	✓

We would highly recommend using a rubric when students are making a booklet. Here is a sample:

Captivates the Reader	• Makes little or no effort to try to hold the readers' attention • Insufficient use of descriptive words to discuss scenery, character studies, actions, or questions	• Makes a limited effort to hold the reader's attention • At times, captivates the reader through meager descriptions of scenery, character studies, actions, or questions	• Makes a reasonable effort at captivating the reader • Is successful to a large measure by using thorough descriptions of scenery, character studies, actions, or questions	• Successfully captivates the reader • Uses highly descriptive and proficient writing: realistic character studies, scenic portrayals, plausible action, and posing questions

Applying the Strategy

Scavenger Hunt can be used in any content area. Just think of having a classroom filled with crystals and hunting for the one that meets the description. Or having items from Salem, Massachusetts that depict the witch hunts that took place in years past while reading *The Crucible*. Even in New Orleans today, stories of ghosts who made their markings can be found throughout the city. In other words, the Scavenger Hunt can be implemented in the classroom, in your town, or even online in a distant country around the world.

Interviewing for Intention

There are many formats of interviews that have been observed. In this case, we will call the interviewer a *host* and the interviewee a *guest*. Students will be able to relate to this identification because of popular television show hosts such as Oprah Winfrey, David Letterman, or Anderson Cooper. The popularity of the television show host will vary depending on the age range of students and popular media. Do not let our recommendation be the benchmark. Choose examples of television hosts you deem appropriate.

Different hosts often specialize in interviewing certain types of guests. For example, on *Behind the Actors Studio*, James Lipton interviews well-known actors. Anderson Cooper is known for his politics. David Letterman often has interesting entertainers from dog trainers to musical groups as his guest. Oprah, on the other hand, has more of a variety show of authors and guests that have played a significant role in social history.

An interview can have the participant explain in detail his or her view of a current situation happening in the world, or it can be a session on how something works, like an invention. Taking a different tactic, giving an interview may consist of having someone reflect on the spoken stories and recollections that are gathered and preserved in the memories of the participants and their descendants, as in an oral history.

There are many ways communication can be established to hear the stories. You can interview the person over the telephone, by letter, by e-mail, by Skype, with other forms of social media, or in person.

How to Do It

Before the interview takes place, students must learn to conduct the proper research. They should familiarize themselves with the individual to be interviewed. Many sources should be utilized from books written by the person or by others, to other forms such as media clips, apps, articles, and blogs. The interview host should recognize that they have to ask questions that they may not necessarily be familiar with, so they need to be properly prepared.

Therefore, we strongly recommend that the teacher-coach begin by showing several different examples of hosts interviewing a guest followed by a discussion of how each interview was conducted.

- In what ways did each interview style differ?
- Was one host more light and social whereas another might have dug into areas that were somewhat uncomfortable?
- Was one host more humorous while another was more heartfelt?
- Did the hosts appear to be well prepared as shown in their line of questioning?

There are many questions that the class can discuss to set the stage for their own inquiry.

Once their research is complete, have students generate a list of questions that they would like to ask their interview guest. Allow them a few minutes to generate the lists alone. Provide students the opportunity to share them with their cooperative group and rate them from the most essential questions to the least essential ones. Depending on the topic, generate a list of areas to consider. Using an interview dealing with the oral history of a person who immigrated to this country, you may use the following guide to help students get started:

- home and community life
- childhood
- personalities
- relationships
- economic conditions
- family traits that many relatives share
- reasons why they or their ancestors left
- a specific description of what he or she remembers of a childhood home
- a description of the subject's neighborhood so that the viewers can see it, hear the different sounds, and even smell it

Students should rewrite their questions so that they are open-ended. In other words, instead of asking, "Whom were you named after?" ask "For what reasons did your parents choose your name?" Describe in detail whom they were named after and for what reasons that person was so endearing. In whole-group format, the class now shares their questions. Record their responses on chart paper.

Ideas for Assessment

Together with students, brainstorm a list of criteria that will be used to assess them. If it is an interview that would be published in a class newspaper, how well was the interview written? In what ways did it flow logically? In other words, what will you be looking for while grading the student's work? What characteristics will other students think are valuable while reading the oral history composition? Some suggestions to consider while developing the criteria assessment are:

- Clarity of writing style: Was it well-developed in either the first person, or third person?

- Does the story captivate the reader in an interesting way?

- Depth of description: Did the student elicit enough information to give a rich and detailed story?

- Multimodal: Did the student include a recording of a song, a video, pictures, and/or memorabilia?

- Layout and design: Did the student make an effort to incorporate different elements with the text in a presentable fashion?

In this case, a rubric may be considered. Here is a sample of one criteria.

Clarity of Written Text	• Writing is difficult to comprehend and is wholly inadequate to what the writer is trying to express. • The text is difficult to read and vague.	• Writing is slightly muddled, lacking clear usage of words. • It presents the reader with some difficulty in following the text.	• Writing is reasonably clear, as most thoughts are described in a complete manner. • Nearly all of the text is comprehended with ease.	• Superb and crystal-clear writing; each word accurately describes the thoughts and intentions of the author. • Easy to follow and understand.

If this were an interview in which the class was the host and a guest speaker came to the class, then a different set of criteria would be used for guidelines.

Applying the Strategy

Interviewing for Intention can be done in any content area. Just read the latest newspaper or *The New York Times* to get your juices flowing. Will students be interviewing the latest fashion designer or architect from the styles section? Will they interview a doctor or a spokesperson from a pharmaceutical lab about genetics? Or will they be interviewing a favorite children's author? In other words, our sample above may have been taken from social studies, but the sky is the limit!

Conclusion

Inquiry is at the heart of learning. When students can make meaning from evidence or research, real learning takes place. This type of learning is not something that is easily forgotten by students. All the strategies in this chapter are inquiry-based. They vary in the implementation or steps, but the outcome is that students learn through questioning and investigations. These strategies include the 5E Model, Project-Based Learning, Research and Investigations, Problem-Based Learning, Creative Problem Solving, and Discovery Learning.

The 5E Model is based on a constructivist philosophy of learning that involves students building or constructing their own understanding of new ideas based on what they already know. It is a model based on *engaging*, *exploring*, *explaining*, *elaborating*, and *evaluating* a particular content or topic. Project-Based Learning has students creating projects to show what they have learned and replaces worksheets with higher-order thinking skills. Research and Investigations teaches students to become reliable and practical researchers, a skill that will eventually span many different kinds of topics. In order to find information in the most efficient ways, students learn proper methods for researching and investigating a topic. Problem-Based Learning is a problem-solving strategy that engages students in solving a lifelike or real-life problem. Direct instruction is limited, and students are given the opportunity to collaborate with their classmates as they study the issues of a certain problem. In effect, students have to take on the responsibility for their own learning. Creative Problem Solving is a problem-solving strategy that uses three main steps to solve a problem. Throughout these steps, students understand the problem, generate ideas, and finally, plan for action. Discovery Learning is an inquiry-based learning method where a teacher-coach sets up an experiment, acts as a coach, and provides clues along the way to help students arrive at solutions. In this way, teacher-coaches provide students with certain tools for learning a concept, and the students make sense of the tools.

Let's Think and Discuss

1. Explain specifically which of the strategies would be the easiest to implement in your classroom, and why.

2. Describe in detail some possible content-related problems or questions that students could investigate.

3. If your students were to use Project-Based Learning, what three or four projects might you have them create to show what they have learned?

Chapter

9

Getting Started with Active Learning

It can be overwhelming to think about how to begin using more active learning strategies in your class. Implementing active learning from a big picture stance will make the strategies most effective for your students. The key is strategic planning. When you know what units you will be studying ahead of time, it is easier to see how these different strategies can fit into your teaching.

To begin, use a calendar to map out your year with general units of study. For example, a kindergarten class might study why families are important in January and February. A sixth-grade class might study the area of triangles, cylinders, and cones during November and December. A ninth-grade biology class might study genetics in March and April. Use a calendar as a visual for planning the year.

After you have your units of study mapped out, decide which strategies in this book will fit best with the different units of study. For example, an Identity Crisis would work well with a unit on elements and features of poetry. Write the selected strategy on the calendar where it will approximately fall within the unit of study. For this example, the teacher might want to use Identity Crisis toward the end of the unit as a review of what students have learned. To truly integrate active learning, make sure each day has one component of active learning.

Then, begin to think about the strategies that activate prior knowledge to use at the beginning of the units or when introducing a new concept during the units. These strategies get students excited about learning and also provide the necessary feedback teachers need so they can differentiate accordingly. For example, True or False Games about the Cold War will assess how much students really know about the topic. A Layered Ball activity will give students extra practice in math with multiplication facts and also work well in language arts in a book study group with questions about a story.

The chart in Figure 9.1 can be used as a unit planner. It asks for a brief summary of the lessons and the active learning strategy that can be applied to teach the lesson. Some of these lessons might take several days to complete, and others will take just one class period. The active learning strategies applied to each lesson should correlate with the days needed. This planning guide is not meant to be static. It should evolve, and modifications should be made according to the needs of students. It is not the expectation that such planning is set in stone. A full-size version of the unit planner can be found in Appendix B.

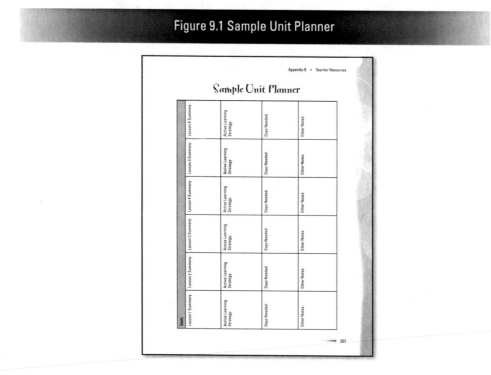

Figure 9.1 Sample Unit Planner

After briefly charting out the entire unit, a teacher will need to be more specific with each particular lesson that uses an active learning strategy. The sample chart in Figure 9.2 can help organize the lesson and the things a teacher will need to do to prepare for that lesson. The full-size lesson organizer can be found in Appendix B.

Figure 9.2 Sample Lesson Organizer

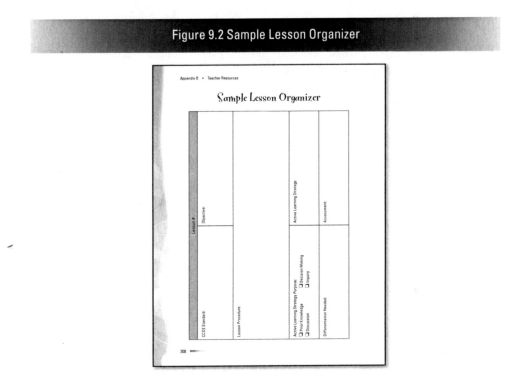

Remember, it is good to repeat the same active learning strategies throughout the year. The first time you implement a strategy, students will have to learn the rules and details to do it. The next time it is implemented, students will catch on much quicker and less time will be spent on instructions. For example, students will better understand how the clerks pass notes during the Stix Discussion when it is used a second time. Students will have developed a better understanding of how to ask good questions the third time they participate in an Identity Crisis activity.

As you embark on this endeavor to make learning more active, take comfort in the fact that your hard work will pay off. Know that you are educating your students in the very best way. And as your students begin to demonstrate their love for learning, you will also renew your love of teaching.

Let's Think and Discuss

1. What goals will you set for using active learning strategies with your students this year?

2. Describe in detail the small steps you will take to get started using active learning strategies.

3. In what ways can you work with your colleagues to implement active learning in your school?

References Cited

Anderson, John R., Lynne M. Reder, and Herbert A. Simon. 1997. *Applications and Misapplications of Cognitive Psychology to Mathematics Education.* Pittsburgh, PA: Carnegie Mellon University.

Asher, James. 2009. *Learning Another Language Through Actions.* Los Gatos, CA: Sky Oak Productions.

Baker, David W. 1989. "Neuropsychology and Appropriate Modes of Instruction." PhD diss., Columbia University.

Baker, Richard A. 2011. The Relationship Between Music and Visual Arts Formal Study and Academic Achievement on the Eighth-Grade Louisiana Educational Assessment Program (LEAP) Test. PhD diss., Louisiana State University.

Ballantine, Joan, and Patricia M. Larres. 2007. "Final Year Accounting Undergraduates' Attitudes to Group Assessment and the Role of Learning Logs." Accounting Education 16: 163–183.

Bass, Kristin M., Danielle Yumol, and Julia Hazer. 2012. "The Effect of Raft Hands-On Activities on Student Learning, Engagement, and 21st Century Skills." RAFT Student Impact Study. Accessed on January 24. http://www.raft.net/public/pdfs/Rockman-RAFT-Report.pdf.

Bransford, J., J. Franks, N. Vye, and R. Sherwood. 1986. "New Approaches to Instruction: Because Wisdom Can't be Taught" Paper presented at a conference on Similarity and Analogy, University of Illinois, Champaign- Urbana.

Bruner, Jerome. 2004. *Toward a Theory of Instruction.* Cambridge, MA: Belnap Press of Harvard University Press.

Bryant, Stephanie M., and James E. Hunton. 2000. "The Use of Technology in the Delivery of Instruction: Implications for Accounting Educators and Education Researchers." *Issues in Accounting Education* 15: 129–163.

Bybee, Rodger., W., Joseph A. Taylor, April Gardner, Pamela Van Scotter, Janet Carlson Powell, Anne Westbrook, and Nancy Lande. 2006. *The BSCS 5E Instructional Model: Origins, Effectiveness, and Applications.* Colorado Springs: BSCS. 2006.

Caine, Renate N., and Geoffrey Caine. 1997. *Education on the Edge of Possibility.* Alexandria, VA: Association for Supervision and Curriculum Development.

Catterall, James S., Richard Chapleau, and John Iwanaga. 1998. "Involvement in the Arts and Human Development: General Involvement and Intensive Involvement in Music and Theatre Arts." *Champions of Change*: 1–18.

Conklin, Wendy. 2004. *Applying Differentiation Strategies.* Huntington Beach, CA: Shell Education.

———. 2006. *Building Fluency through Reader's Theater: Two Flat Friends Travel the World.* Huntington Beach, CA: Teacher Created Materials.

Conklin, Wendy, and Debbie Murphy. 2014. *The How-to Guide for Integrating the Common Core in Language Arts.* Huntington Beach, CA: Shell Education.

Crane, Thomas. 2002. *The Heart of Coaching: Using Transformation Coaching to Create a High-Performance Culture.* San Diego, CA: FTA Press.

Csikszentmihalyi, Mihaly. 1996. *Creativity: Flow and the Psychology of Discovery and Invention.* New York: Harper Collins.

Danielson, Charlotte. 2007. *Enhancing Professional Practice: A Framework for Teaching*, 2nd edition. Alexandria, VA: Association for the Supervision of Curriculum Development.

Danielson, Charlotte. 2011. "The Framework for Teaching." The Danielson Group. http://www.danielsongroup.org

Diamond, Marian, and Janet Hopson. 1998. *Magic Trees of the Mind: How to Nurture Your Child's Intelligence, Creativity, and Healthy Emotions from Birth Through Adolescence.* New York: Dutton.

Donovan, Lisa, and Louise Pascale. 2012. *Integrating the Arts Across the Content Areas*. Huntington Beach, CA: Shell Education.

Fern, Veronica, Kris Anstrom, and Barbara Silcox. 2005. "Active Learning and the Limited English Proficient Student." *Directions in Language and Education National Clearinghouse for Bilingual Education* 1: 3–9.

Gardner, Howard. (1983) 2011. *Frames of Mind: The Theory of Multiple Intelligences*. New York: Basic Books.

———. 1993. *Multiple Intelligences: The Theory in Practice*. New York: Basic Books.

Green, Linda Schwartz, and Diane Casale-Giannola. 2011. *40 Active Learning Strategies for the Inclusive Classroom*. Thousand Oaks, CA: Corwin Press.

Green, Maxine. 1992. "The Passion of Pluralism: Multiculturalism and the Expanding Community." Journal of Negro Education 61: 250–261.

Hannaford, Carla. 1995. *Smart Moves*. Arlington, VA: Great Ocean Publishing Company.

Herreid, Clyde F. 1996. "Structured controversy: A case study strategy." *Journal of College Science Teaching*, 26: 95-101.

Herrell, Adrienne, and Michael Jordan. 2004. *Fifty Strategies for Teaching English Language Learners*. Upper Saddle River, NJ: Pearson.

Ho, Yim-Chi, Agnes S. Chan, and Mei-Chun Cheung. 2003. "Music Training Improves Verbal but not Visual Memory: Cross-Sectional and Longitudinal Explorations in Children." *Neuropsychology*, 17 (3), 439-450.

Jackson, Robyn R. 2009. *Never Work Harder Than Your Students and Other Principles of Great Teaching*. Alexandria, VA: Association for Supervision and Curriculum Development.

Jacobs, Heidi H. 2010. *Curriculum 21: Essential Education for a Changing World*. Alexandria, VA: Association for Supervision and Curriculum Development.

Jensen, Eric. 1998. *Teaching with the Brain in Mind.* Alexandria, VA: Association for Supervision and Curriculum Development.

Kagan, Spencer. 1994. *Cooperative Learning.* San Clemente, CA: Kagan Publishing.

Kise, Jane A. G. 2006. *Differentiated Coaching: A Framework for Helping Teachers Change.* Thousand Oaks, CA: Corwin Press.

Kounin, Jacob S. 1977. *Discipline and Group Management in Classrooms.* Huntington, NH: Krieger.

Larmer, J. and J. R. Mergendoller. 2010. "Seven Essentials for Project-Based Learning." *Educational Leadership* 68 (1): 34-37.

Latrhop, L., Vincent, C., and Annette M. Zehler. 1993. *Special Issues Analysis Center Focus Group Report: Active Learning Instructional Models for Limited English Proficient (LEP) Students.* Report to U.S. Department of Education, Office of Bilingual Education and Minority Languages Affairs (OBEMLA). Arlington, VA: Development Associates, Inc.

Lou, Yiping, Philip C. Abrami, John C. Spence, Catherine Poulsen, Bette Chambers, and Sylvia d'Apollonia. 1996. "Within Class Groupings: A Meta-Analysis." *Review of Educational Research* 66: 423–458.

Marzano, Robert J., Debra J. Pickering, and Jane E. Pollock. 2001. *Classroom Instruction that Works: Research-Based Strategies for Increasing Student Achievement.* Alexandria, VA: Association for Supervision and Curriculum Development.

McGaugh, James L., Larry Cahill, and Benno Roozendaal. 1996. "Involvement of the Amygdala in Memory Storage: Interaction with Other Brain Systems." *Proceedings of the National Academy of Sciences of the United States of America* 93: 13508–13514.

Mehlinger, Howard. 1995. *School Reform in the Information Age.* Bloomington, IN: Indiana University Press.

Michaud, Ellen, and Russell Wild. 1991. *Boost Your Brain Power: A Total Program to Strengthen and Expand Your Most Important Resource*. Emmaus, PA: Rodale Press.Mims, Clif. 2003. "Authentic Learning: A Practical Introduction and Guide for Implementation." *Meridian* 6 (1).

National Governors Association Center for Best Practices, and Council of Chief State School Officers. 2010. "Common Core State Standards." Washington, DC: National Governors Association.

Osborn Alex, F. 1993. Applied Imagination: Principles and Procedures of Creative Problem Solving, 3rd edition. Amherst, MA: Creative Education Foundation.

Paul, Richard and Linda Elder. 2002. *Critical Thinking: Tools for Taking Charge of Your Professional and Personal Life*. Upper Saddle River, NJ: Pearson Education, Inc.

Peterson, Michael, Karen Feathers, and Kim Beloin. 1997. "Inclusive Literacy Learning: Developing a Whole Language Partnership." http://www.wholeschooling.net/WS/WSPress/ArtInclLitLrning.html.

Piaget, Jean. 1954. *The Construction of Reality in the Child*. New York: Basic Books.

———. 1974. *To Understand Is to Invent: The Future of Education*. New York: Grossman.

Raiffa, Howard. 1968. *Decision Analysis: Introductory Lectures on Choices Under Certainty*. Upper Saddle River, NJ: Addison-Wesley.

Richards, Regina. 2008. "Helping Children with Learning Disabilities Understand What They Read." http://www.nasponline.org/resources/reading/ldarticle.pdf.

Roth, LaVonna. 2012. *Brain-Powered Strategies to Engage All Learners*. Huntington Beach, CA: Shell Education.

Silverstein, Lynne B., and Sean Layne. "Defining Arts Integration." 2010. http://artsedge.kennedy-center.org/~/media/ArtsEdgeLessonPrintables/articles/arts-integration/DefiningArtsIntegration.pdf.

Stix, Andi. 2002, "Understanding Scoring Rubrics: A Guide for Teachers." Chapter 7 in *Creating Rubrics Through Negotiable Contracting*, edited by Carol Boston. ERIC Clearinghouse on Assessment & Evaluation, ISBN: 1-886047-04-9

Stix, Andi, and Frank Hrbek. 1999. "A Rubric Bank for Teachers." *The Interactive Classroom*. Accessed on August 14. http://www.andistix.com.

———. 2002. *Exploring History: Ancient Greece*. Huntington Beach, CA: Teacher Created Materials

———. 2006. *Teachers as Classroom Coaches*. Alexandria VA: Association for Supervision and Curriculum Development.

———. 2014. *Active History: American Revolution*. Huntington Beach, CA: Shell Education.

Taba, Hilda, Mary C. Durkin, Jack R. Fraenkel, Anthony H. McNaughton. 1971. *A Teacher's Handbook to Elementary Social Studies: An Inductive Approach*, 2nd ed. Reading, MA: Addison-Wesley.

Teele, Sue. 1994. "Redesigning the Educational System to Enable All Students to Succeed." PhD diss., University of California, Riverside.

Treffinger, Donald J., Scott G. Isaken, and K. Brian Stead-Dorval. 2006. *Creative Problem Solving: An Introduction*. Waco, TX: Prufrock Press.

Udvari-Solner, Alice, and Paula M. Kluth. 2008. *Joyful Learning: Active and Collaborateive Learning in Inclusive Classrooms*. Thousand Oaks, CA: Corwin.

Von Winterfeldt, Detlof and Ward Edwards. 1986. *Decision Analysis and Behavioral Research*. New York: Cambridge University Press.

Vygotsky, Lev. 1978. *Mind In Society: The Development of Higher Psychological Processes*. Cambridge, MA: Harvard University Press.

Willingham, Dan T. 2009. *Why Don't Students Like School: A Cognitive Scientist Answers Questions About How the Mind Works and What It Means for the Classroom*. San Francisco, CA: Jossey-Bass.

Willis, Judy. 2008. *How Your Child Learns Best: Brain-Friendly Strategies You Can Use to Ignite Your Child's Learning and Increase School Success.* Naperville, IL: Sourcebooks, Inc.

Wishart, Jocelyn, and Derek Blease. 1999. "Theories Underlying Perceived Changes in Teaching and Learning After Installing a Computer Network in a Secondary School." *British Journal of Educational Technology* 30: 25–42.

Zmuda, Allison. 2008. "Springing into Active Learning." *Educational Leadership* 66 (3): 38–42.

The GOPER Assessment Form

Names of Students, Team Name, or Table Number:
Topic:

G: Has the group established their goal(s)? What is their goal or are they still brainstorming?
Date:
Date:

O: In what ways do they have a good comprehension of their options?
Date:
Date:

P: Describe in detail their plan of action:
Date:
Date:

E: Do they have any roadblocks, and if so, describe specifically how they are handling them:
Date:
Date:

R: Explain whether or not the group examines and reflects upon their actions as they move along. In what ways did they learn from working with one another or from accomplishing this project or task?
Date:
Date:

Dates Completed	Goal	Options	Plan of Action	Eliminate the Roadblocks	Reflection

Comments and Reminders:
Date:
Date:

Multiple Intelligences Inventory

Directions: Read each box. Color the ones that tell what you like.

I like . . .

writing stories	telling stories	reading	spelling	doing searches
math problems	counting	playing checkers	measuring things	making graphs
playing instruments	humming tunes	writing songs	listening to music	singing
puzzles	drawing	painting	making sculptures	looking at maps
playing sports	hiking	acting	moving around	dancing
playing games	group work	being the leader	talking to people	talking on the phone
keeping a journal	setting goals	thinking	time alone	reading alone
the outdoors	learing about weather	nature	animals	watching animals

Socratic Method: Student Assessment Chart

Topic:	Listening and Responding	Adding New Information	Analyzing Peer Comments	Good Eye Contact	Date:	Listening and Responding	Adding New Information	Analyzing Peer Comments	Good Eye Contact
Student's Name:									
1.					15.				
2.					16.				
3.					17.				
4.					18.				
5.					19.				
6.					20.				
7.					21.				
8.					22.				
9.					23.				
10.					24.				
11.					25.				
12.					26.				
13.					27.				
14.					28.				

Sample Unit Planner

Unit:					
Lesson 1 Summary:	Lesson 2 Summary:	Lesson 3 Summary:	Lesson 4 Summary:	Lesson 5 Summary:	Lesson 6 Summary:
Active Learning Strategy:	Active Learning Strategy:	Active Learning Strategy:	Active Learning Strategy:	Active Learning Strategy:	Active Learning Strategy:
Days Needed:	Days Needed:	Days Needed:	Days Needed:	Days Needed:	Days Needed:
Other Notes:	Other Notes:	Other Notes:	Other Notes:	Other Notes:	Other Notes:

Sample Lesson Organizer

Lesson #			
CCSS Standard:	Objective:	Active Learning Strategy:	Assessment:
	Lesson Procedure:		
		Active Learning Strategy Purpose: ☐ Prior Knowledge ☐ Decision Making ☐ Discussion ☐ Inquiry	Differentiation Needed: